Decoding Antiquity

Volume Two

Translating Ancient Texts

Unlocking the past

John A Gillam

Independent Writer On Antiquity

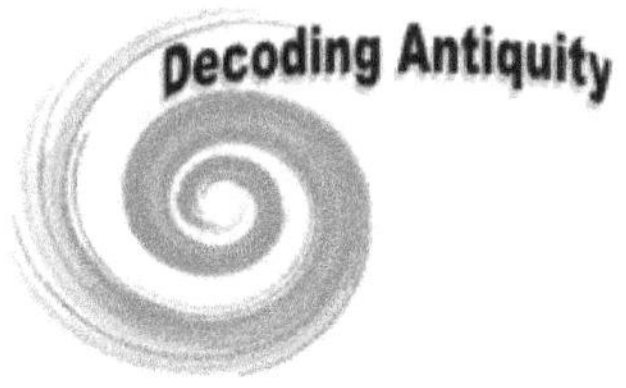

Table of Contents

PUBLICATION DETAILS

Cover illustration AI generated by John Gillam using Microsoft Designer.

First edition October 2024

Published by Decoding Antiquity, Canberra.

A division of Creative Horizons Healthcare. ABN 87 866 904 801.

www.decodingantiquity.weebly.com

ACKNOWLEDGMENTS

I express my gratitude to all those who supported and inspired me throughout the writing of this book. To my wife and friends, thank you for your encouragement. To the readers of this book, thank you for your interest in translating ancient texts.

I also extend my heartfelt appreciation to the numerous authors and researchers whose works I have referenced throughout this book. Your dedication and the sharing of your knowledge has been invaluable to my own research and writing processes. Without your tireless efforts and insightful contributions, this book would not have been possible.

To all the scholars, archaeologists, linguists, historians, librarians, museum curators, and scientists who are concerned with the deciphering and translation of ancient scripts, I am deeply grateful. Your commitment to rigorous research, evidence-based analysis, and document preservation has been a constant source of inspiration and guidance.

In crafting this book, I benefited from the assistance of AI language models, which provided valuable research support and creative input.

PREFACE

In museums, libraries, and archives around the world, a quiet revolution is unfolding. Dedicated scholars and innovative technologies are bringing the voices of our ancient ancestors to life, deciphering ancient scripts that have remained silent for millennia, and translating the texts lying in wait. This book is your invitation to explore this fascinating world of discovery and learn about the remarkable work being done in the field of ancient text translation.

You will learn about the cutting-edge technologies that are revolutionizing how we read ancient documents, from multispectral imaging that reveals invisible text to artificial intelligence that helps decipher unknown scripts, and fill-in missing text on tablets and parchments.

As you read, you'll gain a new appreciation for the power of the written word to transcend time and connect us with our ancestors. You'll understand why the work of translating ancient texts is so crucial to our understanding of ourselves and our world.

Whether you're a history enthusiast, a language lover, or simply curious about the world around you, this book offers a fascinating glimpse into a field that is constantly evolving and always exciting. Prepare to be amazed by the work being done to bring ancient voices to modern ears, and to uncover the hidden knowledge that could reshape our understanding of the world and our place within it.

John A. Gillam

GLOSSARY

Agglutinative: A type of language where words are formed by stringing together morphemes, each of which represents a single grammatical meaning.

Akkadian: An extinct East Semitic language that was the lingua franca of the Ancient Near East.

Alphabet: A writing system in which each symbol represents a consonant or vowel sound.

Amate paper: A type of paper made from bark, used in pre-Columbian Mesoamerica.

Bilingual text: A text written in two different languages, often used to help decipher unknown scripts.

Codex (pl. Codices): An ancient manuscript text in book form, particularly referring to Maya books.

Cuneiform: A writing system developed in ancient Mesopotamia using wedge-shaped marks on clay tablets.

Decipherment: The process of figuring out how to read a previously unknown writing system.

Demotic: A script used for writing the Egyptian language during the latter part of ancient Egyptian history.

Determinative: A sign used to clarify the meaning of a word by indicating its semantic category.

Epigraphy: The study of inscriptions or epigraphs as writing.

Hieroglyphs: A formal writing system used by the ancient Egyptians that combined logographic and alphabetic elements.

Ideogram: A graphic symbol that represents an idea or concept.

Isolate language: A language that has no demonstrated genetic relationship with any other known language.

Lexicography: The process of compiling, writing, and editing dictionaries.

Ligature: A character consisting of two or more joined letters; eg, 'æ'.

Linear A: An undeciphered writing system used in ancient Crete.

Linear B: A syllabic script used for writing Mycenaean Greek.

Logogram: A written character that represents a word or morpheme.

Logosyllabic: A writing system that uses both logograms and syllabic signs.

Maya script: A logosyllabic writing system developed by the Maya civilization of Mesoamerica.

Microbiome: The collective community of microorganisms that inhabited the bodies and environments of people.

Orthography: The conventional spelling system of a language.

Palimpsest: a manuscript or piece of writing material on which later writing has been superimposed or effaced earlier writing

Philology: The study of language in written historical sources.

Phonogram: A symbol representing a sound or group of sounds.

Pictograph: A pictorial symbol for a word or phrase.

Proto-Elamite: The earliest known writing system of ancient Iran, still largely undeciphered.

Punic: Refers to the people and language of the Carthaginians. The language and script are similar to Modern Hebrew..

Rosetta Stone: An ancient Egyptian artifact inscribed with a decree in three scripts — hieroglyphic, Demotic, and Greek — that enabled the modern decipherment of Egyptian hieroglyphs.

TRANSLATING ANCIENT TEXTS

Scribe: A person who writes out documents or copies text, especially a specialized profession in ancient societies.

Script: A writing system in terms of a specific set of symbols used to represent the sounds of a language.

Stele (pl. Stelae): An upright stone slab or pillar bearing an inscription or design, often used as a monument.

Syllabary: A set of written symbols that represent syllables.

Syllabogram: A written character that represents a syllable.

Transliteration: The process of transferring a text from one writing system into another.

Ventive: In Akkadian, a verbal suffix indicating motion towards the speaker or purpose/intent.

X-ray phase-contrast tomography: An advanced imaging technique using high-energy X-rays to create detailed 3D images of an object's internal structure by detecting subtle density differences, allowing for non-invasive examination of fragile artifacts like ancient scrolls.

◉

CHAPTER ONE

Ancient texts waiting to be deciphered and translated

Language is the archive of history, Ralph Waldo, 'Letters and social aims'. [1]

For millennia, the written word has been humanity's primary tool for preserving knowledge, culture, and history. From the earliest cuneiform tablets of Mesopotamia to the intricate hieroglyphs of ancient Egypt, our ancestors left behind a vast treasure trove of information, waiting to be deciphered and understood [1]. Yet, despite centuries of scholarly efforts, countless ancient texts remain unread, their secrets locked away in languages and scripts that have long fallen silent.

This book, *Translating Ancient Texts*, aims to explore the fascinating world of ancient language decipherment and translation, focusing on texts dating from the 16th century BCE to the 15th century CE. We will delve into the most significant ancient languages believed to contain crucial information for our modern world, examining the challenges faced by scholars, and the exciting potential of artificial intelligence (AI) in unlocking these linguistic puzzles.

The importance of ancient texts

Ancient texts offer us a window into the minds of our ancestors, providing insights into their daily lives, beliefs, and knowledge. These texts can:

- Reveal lost technological advancements
- Uncover forgotten medical treatments
- Expose philosophical ideas that may still hold relevance today
- Contain historical accounts that can fill gaps in our understanding of past events
- Shed light on the rise and fall of civilizations
- Illuminate the movement of peoples
- Trace the development of ideas.

For instance, the discovery and translation of the *Rosetta Stone* in the early 19th century unlocked the secrets of Egyptian hieroglyphs, leading to a renaissance in our understanding of ancient Egyptian culture and history [2]. Similarly, the decipherment of Linear B script in the mid-20th century revealed the earliest known form of Greek, providing crucial insights into Mycenaean civilization [3].

The challenge of untranslated texts

Despite the efforts of generations of linguists, archaeologists, and historians, a vast number of ancient texts remain undeciphered and untranslated. This backlog exists for several reasons:

- <u>Unknown languages</u>: Many ancient scripts represent languages that have no known descendants or relatives, making them extremely difficult to decipher without a *Rosetta Stone* equivalent.
- <u>Lack of context</u>: Often, texts are found with little archaeological context, making it challenging to infer their content or purpose.
- <u>Fragmentation</u>: Many ancient texts have survived only in fragments, making it difficult to piece together coherent meanings.
- <u>Shortage of experts</u>: There are simply not enough scholars with the specialized knowledge required to work on every known ancient language and script.
- <u>Time constraints</u>: Traditional methods of translation are time-consuming, limiting the number of texts that can be processed.

Ancient texts, written in languages long forgotten, often exist as cryptic puzzles for modern scholars. Deciphering these texts involves unraveling the underlying script or language system. This process can be incredibly challenging, requiring the identification of individual characters, understanding their phonetic values, and reconstructing the grammar and syntax of the language.

Once deciphered, the text can then be translated into a modern language, which involves rendering the meaning of the original text as accurately and comprehensibly as possible. However, translation is not always a straightforward task, as cultural nuances, historical context, and ambiguities in the original text can make it difficult to convey the full meaning. Despite these challenges, the decipherment and translation of ancient texts provide invaluable insights into the history, culture, and thoughts of past civilizations.

Several ancient languages have a wealth of documents (tablets, papyri, scrolls, etc) that remain untranslated in museums and archives worldwide. We will look at the following languages as being some of the most fascinating ones from historical, cultural, and linguistic interest:

- **Sumerian** — from circa 3100 BCE

Sumerian is one of the earliest known written languages, originating in Mesopotamia (modern-day Iraq). There are tens of thousands of cuneiform tablets in various museums around the world that contain administrative records, legal texts, literature, and more, mostly remaining to be translated. The key to deciphering Sumerian was the discovery of bilingual texts written in both Sumerian and Akkadian. By comparing the two versions of these texts, scholars were able to gradually unravel the Sumerian language system.

- **Egyptian Hieroglyphs and Demotic Script** — from circa 3100 BCE

The Egyptian language, particularly in its hieroglyphic and demotic forms, was used for millennia in various inscriptions and manuscripts. Large numbers of papyri and inscriptions remain untranslated, many housed in museums like the Egyptian Museum in Cairo and the British Museum.

Both the Egyptian hieroglyphics and the demotic script have been deciphered and translated. The breakthrough came with the discovery of the *Rosetta Stone* in 1799, a trilingual inscription in ancient Egyptian hieroglyphs, demotic script, and ancient Greek. The Greek text provided a key to understanding the other two scripts. Jean-François Champollion is credited with the final decipherment of hieroglyphs in the early 19th century. He realized that hieroglyphs could represent sounds, not just ideas, and used the *Rosetta Stone* and other known hieroglyphic inscriptions to decode the script. The demotic script, a simplified form of hieroglyphs, was also deciphered using the *Rosetta Stone* and other parallel texts. While it took slightly longer to fully understand, it was eventually deciphered and translated.

- **Akkadian** — from circa 2500 BCE

Akkadian is another ancient language from Mesopotamia, closely related to Sumerian, and was written in the cuneiform script. There are thousands of Akkadian tablets, including royal inscriptions, legal documents, and letters, yet to be fully translated.

The process of deciphering Akkadian began in the 19th century, thanks to the discovery of bilingual inscriptions (written in both Akkadian and a known language like Old Persian). Scholars like Edward Hincks, Henry Rawlinson and Jules Oppert played crucial roles in this process. By comparing the known language with the unknown Akkadian, they were able to gradually decipher the Akkadian script and language.

- **Elamite** — from circa 2600 BCE

Elamite was spoken in what is now southwestern Iran from about 2600 BCE to 300 CE. Many administrative and legal documents, royal inscriptions, and bilingual inscriptions with Akkadian remain untranslated.

In 2022, a team of researchers announced a significant breakthrough in deciphering Linear Elamite. By comparing Elamite inscriptions with those written in cuneiform, they were able to identify many characters and words in Linear Elamite. While the decipherment is still ongoing, and there are some remaining challenges, it represents a major step forward in understanding the history and language of the Elamite people.

- **Indus Valley Script** — from circa 2600 BCE

The script of the Indus Valley Civilization (c. 2600-1900 BCE) remains undeciphered. Thousands of seals and tablets with the Indus Valley script have been discovered, primarily in modern-day Pakistan and India. The script is unlike any other known writing system, making it challenging to identify potential connections or influences.

- **Linear B and Linear A** — from circa 1450 BCE

Linear B is a syllabic script used for writing Mycenaean Greek, while Linear A remains undeciphered and was used by the Minoan civilization on Crete. Linear B was deciphered and translated in 1952 by Michael Ventris, a British architect, who identified it as an early form of Greek, specifically Mycenaean Greek. This breakthrough provided invaluable insights into the history and culture of the Mycenaean civilization. Linear A is believed to be a non-Indo-European language, possibly related to the Minoan civilization's unique culture and mythology.

- **Ancient Greek** — from circa 1500 BCE

The Ancient Greek script and language, with roots tracing back to the Mycenaean Linear B script of the 2nd millennium BCE, evolved into the familiar Greek alphabet around the 8th century BCE. This writing system remained in use for over two millennia, profoundly shaping Western civilization. Ancient Greek was the lingua franca of philosophy, science, and literature in the classical world, producing a vast corpus of works that continue to influence modern thought. While the language has been fully deciphered and extensively studied, the sheer volume of surviving texts — estimated at over

100 million words across tens of thousands of documents — means that ongoing translation efforts persist. Major collections of Ancient Greek texts are housed in institutions like the National Library of Greece in Athens, the British Library in London, and the Vatican Library in Rome, with countless smaller collections scattered globally.

- **Phoenician** — from circa 1050 BCE

Phoenician was a Semitic language spoken by the ancient Phoenicians, who were known for their maritime trading empire. The Phoenician script has been deciphered and translated. The Phoenician alphabet, one of the earliest known alphabetic writing systems, was deciphered in the 18th century. It was instrumental in the development of subsequent alphabets, including the Greek, Latin, and Cyrillic scripts. While many Phoenician inscriptions have been deciphered, the complete translation of all Phoenician texts remains an ongoing task. Some texts are fragmentary or damaged, and the full context of certain words or phrases may be unclear. However, significant progress has been made in understanding the Phoenician language and culture through the study of these inscriptions.

- **Etruscan** — from circa 700 BCE

Etruscan was the language of the ancient Etruscan civilization in Italy before the rise of Rome. There are numerous inscriptions on tombstones, ceramics, and other artifacts, many of which remain untranslated. Etruscan script has been partially deciphered, but a complete translation remains elusive. While scholars have made significant progress in understanding the Etruscan alphabet and some basic words and phrases, the language itself remains largely mysterious. The limited number of surviving texts and inscriptions, combined with the complexity of the Etruscan script, has made it difficult to fully grasp the grammar, syntax, and meaning of the language.

- **Maya Hieroglyphs** — from circa 200 CE

The Maya script, used in Mesoamerica from 200-900 CE, is a complex system of glyphs representing both sounds and words. They have mostly been deciphered. Hundreds of stelae, codices, and other inscriptions still exist, many in Central American museums, some of which remain partially or fully untranslated.

Even in those languages which have been deciphered, countless documents remain untranslated due to the sheer volume of material and the limited number of experts available to work on them [4] [5].

The promise of AI in ancient text translation

As we stand on the brink of a new era in ancient text decipherment and translation, the possibilities are both exciting and humbling. Artificial intelligence offers a revolutionary approach to the challenge of understanding ancient texts. AI technologies, particularly machine learning and natural language processing, have the potential to dramatically accelerate the process of deciphering and translating ancient texts [7].

Here are some of the key areas where AI is making progress:

- Pattern recognition: AI excels at identifying patterns in data, a crucial skill for deciphering unknown scripts.
- Cross-linguistic comparison: AI can quickly compare unknown texts with vast databases of known languages, potentially identifying similarities that could aid in translation.
- Reconstruction of damaged texts: Machine learning algorithms can be trained to predict missing characters or words in damaged texts, based on context and known patterns in the language.
- Handling volume: AI can process enormous amounts of text far more quickly than human translators, potentially working through

backlogs of untranslated material in a fraction of the time it would take traditional scholars.

- Continuous learning: As more texts are translated, AI systems can update their knowledge and improve their accuracy over time, becoming increasingly sophisticated in their understanding of ancient languages.

Current progress in AI-assisted translation

Several promising projects are already underway, showcasing the potential of AI in this field:

- The DeepMind AI system has shown remarkable success in restoring and translating damaged ancient Greek texts [8]. DeepMind, an artificial intelligence research lab, has made significant strides in the restoration and translation of damaged ancient Greek texts. Their AI system is designed to predict missing portions of texts by analyzing patterns in known Greek manuscripts. It employs machine learning techniques to fill in gaps where the original text is lost or eroded, helping scholars to recover and reconstruct historical writings. The AI system not only restores missing sections but also provides accurate translations of the reconstructed content. This breakthrough could revolutionize the study of ancient languages, allowing historians and linguists to access previously indecipherable or incomplete texts with unprecedented accuracy and speed.
- Researchers at MIT and Google have developed an AI system that can decipher lost languages [9]. Using machine learning algorithms, the system analyzes linguistic patterns in both known and unknown languages, drawing on vast datasets to detect similarities and structural rules. The project focuses on decoding languages that lack direct modern descendants or have no known translations. By identifying recurring patterns, the AI can help linguists piece together the meanings of these ancient languages, potentially unlocking new insights into forgotten cultures and civilizations. This system holds promise for recovering knowledge from ancient texts

that have remained enigmatic for centuries.

- The Glyph project, a collaboration between several universities, is using machine learning to analyze Maya hieroglyphs [10]. This project seeks to decipher and analyze the intricate system of symbols used by the Maya civilization, many of which remain poorly understood. By training AI models on known hieroglyphic inscriptions, the system can recognize patterns, suggest possible meanings for unknown symbols, and assist in the translation of ancient texts. The Glyph project not only speeds up the process of understanding Maya writing but also helps preserve this cultural heritage by making it more accessible to scholars and the public. This initiative could transform the field of Mesoamerican studies by providing a deeper understanding of Maya language and culture.

These examples represent just the beginning of AI's potential in this field. As technology advances and more data becomes available, we can expect even more impressive breakthroughs in the coming years.

The potential contents of untranslated texts

While we cannot know for certain what information lies hidden in untranslated texts, based on what we've learned from previously deciphered writings, we can speculate on some possibilities:

- <u>Historical records</u>: Many ancient texts contain chronicles of rulers, wars, and significant events.
- <u>Scientific and medical knowledge</u>: Ancient civilizations often possessed sophisticated understanding of mathematics, astronomy, and medicine.
- <u>Philosophical and religious ideas</u>: Ancient texts often contain complex philosophical or theological discussions.
- <u>Literary works</u>: Epic poems, stories, and other forms of literature can offer insights into ancient societies.
- <u>Economic and administrative records</u>: These texts can provide valuable information about ancient social structures, trade networks,

and economic systems.

- <u>Technological information</u>: Some texts might contain information about lost technologies or engineering techniques.
- <u>Astronomical observations</u>: Ancient civilizations often kept detailed records of celestial events.

The potential value of this information to our current society is immense. Historical records could help us better understand the rise and fall of civilizations, potentially offering lessons for our own societies. Ancient scientific knowledge might provide new directions for modern research or rediscover effective treatments lost to time. Philosophical texts could offer fresh perspectives on age-old questions of ethics, governance, and the human condition.

Location of untranslated texts

Untranslated ancient texts can be found in various locations around the world, including:

- <u>Museums</u>: Major institutions like the British Museum, the Louvre, and the Egyptian Museum in Cairo.
- <u>Libraries</u>: Specialized libraries such as the Vatican Apostolic Library or the Library of Alexandria.
- <u>Archaeological sites</u>: Ongoing excavations continue to unearth new texts.
- <u>Private collections</u>: Some important texts are held in private collections.
- <u>Digital archives</u>: Increasingly, ancient texts are being digitized and made available online.

Some specific examples of locations with significant collections of untranslated texts include:

- <u>The Oxyrhynchus Papyri</u>: A vast collection of over 500,000 papyrus fragments from ancient Egypt dating from the third century BCE. Housed at the University of Oxford [11].

- <u>The Dead Sea Scrolls</u>: Ancient Jewish texts, many fragments of which remain untranslated or disputed. There are some 100,000 fragments made on animal skin, papyrus, and copper. They are housed in the Shrine of the Book at the Israel Museum in Jerusalem [12].
- <u>The Villa dei Papiri</u>: Some 1,800 papyrus scrolls written in Ancient Greek were discovered at this ancient Roman villa in Herculaneum. These scrolls, carbonized by the volcanic eruption of Mount Vesuvius in 79 CE, have been the subject of great interest and ongoing research. Many remain unread due to their fragile condition, though modern technologies are being employed to decipher their contents without damaging them. The majority of these scrolls are now housed in the National Library of Naples (Biblioteca Nazionale di Napoli) in Italy [13].

X-ray phase-contrast tomography has been used to reveal the hidden text within many of the carbonized Herculaneum papyri without physically unrolling them. This non-invasive technique employs high-energy X-rays to detect minute differences in density between the charred papyrus and the ink, creating detailed 3D images of the scrolls' internal structure. By virtually 'unrolling' these images, researchers can read the ancient text that has been concealed for nearly two millennia. The method was first successfully applied to the Herculaneum scrolls in 2015, allowing scholars to decipher Greek letters and words from the fragile artifacts. Since then, the technique has been refined to improve resolution and distinguish between different types of characters. Beyond the Herculaneum papyri, this technology has been adapted for use in other archaeological contexts, such as examining the contents of sealed ancient Egyptian canopic jars and studying delicate fossils. The success of this method has opened up new possibilities for uncovering and preserving historical information from fragile or damaged artifacts that were previously considered unreadable [14].

- <u>The Dunhuang manuscripts</u>: A collection of over 600,000 manuscripts and documents from the Mogao Caves at Dunhuang in China. They are primarily written in Chinese, but also Tibetan, Sanskrit, Sogdian, Uighur, and other languages, dating from the 5th to 11th centuries AD. They are mostly housed at the National Library of China and the Dunhuang Academy. Smaller collections are held at the British Library, and the Bibliothèque nationale de France [15].

The following illustrations are from Wikipedia:

Oxyrhynchus Papyri

Dead Sea Scrolls.
(Temple Scroll)

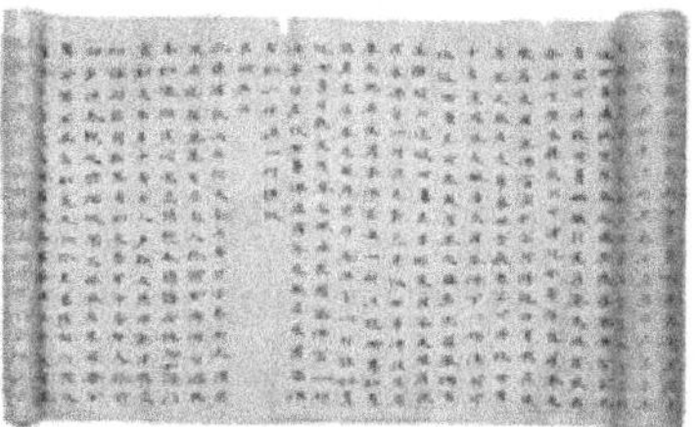

Dunhuang manuscripts

Accuracy of existing translations

When discussing ancient text translation, it's crucial to address the accuracy of existing translations. Several factors can affect the accuracy of translations:

- <u>Limited context</u>: Often, translators must work with fragmentary texts or limited contextual information.
- <u>Evolution of language understanding</u>: As our knowledge of ancient languages grows, earlier translations may be revised.
- <u>Cultural differences</u>: Ancient texts often reference cultural concepts or idioms that may not have direct modern equivalents.
- <u>Bias</u>: Translators may interpret texts through the lens of their own cultural or personal biases.
- <u>Lack of standardization</u>: Ancient languages often lack standardized grammar or spelling.

The case of Zecharia Sitchin's work is a prime example of the controversies that can arise in this field. Sitchin's translations and interpretations of Sumerian texts have been strongly criticized by mainstream scholars. They argue that Sitchin's work constitutes pseudoscience, citing his selective use of sources and literal interpretation of mythological texts. Despite these criticisms, Sitchin's ideas have gained a significant popular following, though they remain outside mainstream academic acceptance. [16].

The role of AI in improving translation accuracy

Artificial intelligence has the potential to significantly improve the accuracy of ancient text translations in several ways:

- <u>Consistency</u>: AI can apply translation rules consistently across large volumes of text.
- <u>Pattern recognition</u>: AI can identify subtle linguistic patterns that might be missed by human translators.
- <u>Cross-referencing</u>: AI can quickly compare a text with a vast database of other translated works.
- <u>Probability analysis</u>: Machine learning models can provide probability distributions for different possible translations.
- <u>Continuous improvement</u>: AI systems can continuously refine their understanding and improve their translation capabilities.

Conclusion

As we unlock the contents of ancient texts, we take another step towards the maturity of our species, gaining a deeper appreciation of our shared human heritage and the long journey that has brought us to where we are today. The untapped knowledge contained in undeciphered scripts and untranslated documents promises to reshape our understanding of human history, culture, and thought.

The chapters that follow will delve into the specifics of major ancient languages, exploring their unique challenges and the progress being made in deciphering and translating these languages. As we uncover the voices of our ancestors, we may find not only answers to long-standing questions but also new queries that challenge our understanding of ourselves and our place in the long continuum of human history. The translation of ancient texts is more than an academic exercise; it is a bridge across time, connecting us with the thoughts, dreams, and wisdom of those who came before us.

<u>References</u>

[1] Emerson, R. W. (1876). *Letters and Social Aims*. James R. Osgood and Company.

[2] Daniels, P. T., & Bright, W. (1996). *The World's Writing Systems*. Oxford University Press.

[3] Parkinson, R. (1999). *Cracking Codes: The Rosetta Stone and Decipherment*. University of California Press.

[4] Chadwick, J. (1990). *The Decipherment of Linear B*. Cambridge University Press.

[5] Bonfante, L., & Bonfante, G. (2002). *The Etruscan Language: An Introduction*. Manchester University Press.

[6] Robinson, A. (2009). *Lost Languages: The Enigma of the World's Undeciphered Scripts*. Thames & Hudson.

[7] Roued-Cunliffe, H., & Copeland, A. (Eds.). (2017). *Participatory Heritage*. Facet Publishing.

[8] Assael, Y., Sommerschield, T., & Prag, J. (2022). Restoring and attributing ancient texts using deep neural networks. *Nature*, 603(7900), 280-283.

[9] Luo, J., Cao, Y., & Barzilay, R. (2019). Neural Decipherment via Minimum-Cost Flow: From Ugaritic to Linear B. *arXiv preprint arXiv*:1906.06718.

[10] Magli, E., Gronemann, C., Orsini, R., Macdonald, B., Giancarlo, R., & Tamassia, R. (2021). A computational approach to the analysis of Maya glyphs. In *APA& if we are citing a journal article, is it the article title or the journal name that gets italicized?*, 11(1), 1-12.

[11] Bowman, A. K., Coles, R. A., Gonis, N., Obbink, D., & Parsons, P. J. (Eds.). (2007). *Oxyrhynchus: A City and its Texts*. Egypt Exploration Society.

[12] VanderKam, J. C., & Flint, P. (2005). *The Meaning of the Dead Sea Scrolls: Their Significance for Understanding the Bible, Judaism, Jesus, and Christianity*. A&C Black.

[13] Sider, D. (2005). *The Library of the Villa dei Papiri at Herculaneum*. Getty Publications.

[14] Mocella, V., Brun, E., Ferrero, C., & Delattre, D. (2015). Revealing letters in rolled Herculaneum papyri by X-ray phase-contrast imaging. *Nature Communications*, 6, 5895

[15] Rong, X. (2013). *Eighteen Lectures on Dunhuang* (Vol. 5). Brill.

[16] Giunta, J. (2024). Zecharia Sitchin and the Mistranslation of Sumerian Texts. *Ancientpedia*. < ancientpedia.com/zecharia-sitchin-and-the-mistranslation-of-sumerian-texts/>

◎

CHAPTER TWO

Sumerian language and script

The Sumerians were the first to write. They invented the cuneiform script, the earliest known form of writing, and the world's oldest identifiable written language. Their writing was a reflection of their society, their beliefs, and their way of life.

Samuel Noah Kramer, 'History Begins at Sumer: Thirty-Nine Firsts in Recorded History'. [1]

The Sumerians were the first to write. They invented the cuneiform script, the earliest known form of writing, and the world's oldest identifiable written language. Their writing was a reflection of their society, their beliefs, and their way of life [1].

Origins and significance

The Sumerian language, originating in ancient Mesopotamia (modern-day southern Iraq), was the tongue of the Sumer civilization that flourished from approximately 4500 BCE to 1750 BCE [1]. What sets Sumerian apart in the linguistic landscape is its status as an isolate language, meaning it has no known genetic relationship to any other language, living or extinct [2]. This unique characteristic has intrigued linguists and historians for centuries, presenting both challenges and opportunities for our understanding of human language development.

The development of the Sumerian script, known as cuneiform, around 3200 BCE marks a pivotal moment in human history. Considered the earliest writing system in the world, cuneiform derives its name from the Latin word 'cuneus', meaning 'wedge', a reference to the distinctive wedge-shaped impressions made by a reed stylus on wet clay tablets [3].

Cuneiform tablet — Pexels: Kütükoğlu

Geographical distribution and evolution

The Sumerian civilization primarily used their language and script in the southern part of Mesopotamia, in an area known as Sumer. This region encompassed several city-states, each playing a significant role in the development and use of the Sumerian language. Notable among these were Ur, Uruk, Lagash, and Nippur [4]. The use of Sumerian spans an impressive period of over 3,000 years, from its earliest attested writings around 3000 BCE to its last known uses in the 1st century CE [5].

Linguistic features and complexities

One of the most intriguing aspects of the Sumerian language is its complex grammatical structure. Sumerian is classified as an agglutinative language, meaning that grammatical elements are added to the root word as suffixes. This linguistic feature results in long, complex words that can express ideas that would require entire phrases in other languages [6].

Another fascinating feature of Sumerian is its use of determinatives - signs that indicate the category to which a word belongs. These determinatives were not pronounced but served as visual cues to help readers understand the context of the word [7].

Numerical system and mathematical concepts

The Sumerian approach to numbers and mathematics is equally intriguing. Their number system was sexagesimal (base-60), a system that has left its mark on our modern world through our timekeeping and angular measurement systems [8]. We still divide hours into 60 minutes and minutes into 60 seconds, as well as in the 360 degrees of a circle. Additionally, many astronomical calculations still use sexagesimal units, and some financial markets like bonds sometimes use base-60 fractions. The system's main advantage is its high divisibility, making it useful for precise measurements and calculations involving fractions. Its continued use in these areas demonstrates the lasting impact of ancient Sumerian mathematics on our modern world.

The Sumerian textual corpus

The corpus of Sumerian texts is vast and diverse. It is estimated that over one million cuneiform tablets have been excavated, with a significant portion of them in Sumerian [9]. The content of Sumerian texts covers a wide range of topics, providing a comprehensive view of Sumerian society and culture [10].

Literary texts constitute an important category within the Sumerian corpus. These include myths, epics, hymns, and proverbs that offer a window into Sumerian religious beliefs, cultural values, and worldviews. Famous examples include the *Epic of Gilgamesh*, which although better known in its later Akkadian version, has Sumerian origins. Other notable literary works include the *Debate between Bird and Fish* and the *Instructions of Shuruppak*.

Legal texts include law codes, such as the *Code of Ur-Nammu*, which predates the more famous *Code of Hammurabi*. Contract tablets, court proceedings, and other legal documents provide insights into Sumerian concepts of justice, property rights, and social norms.

The corpus also includes a variety of religious and ritual texts. These range from incantations and prayers to detailed descriptions of religious ceremonies and rituals. Such texts are invaluable for understanding Sumerian religious practices and beliefs, including their pantheon of gods and the role of temples in Sumerian society.

Lastly, the corpus contains numerous scholarly and scientific texts. These include mathematical tablets demonstrating advanced understanding of geometry and algebra, astronomical observations, and medical texts describing various ailments and treatments. As Veldhuis [10] notes in his comprehensive study of the cuneiform lexical tradition, these texts reveal the sophisticated intellectual traditions of the Sumerians and their contributions to various fields of knowledge.

Literary achievements: *The Epic of Gilgamesh*

One of the most famous Sumerian texts is the *Epic of Gilgamesh*, which is considered the earliest surviving great work of literature [11]. It follows the journey of Gilgamesh, a demigod king, as he grapples with the death of his friend Enkidu and seeks immortality. Through Gilgamesh's experiences, the epic addresses themes of hubris, the value of human accomplishment in the face of inevitable death, and the importance of leaving a lasting legacy. This timeless narrative continues to resonate with readers, offering insights into the human condition and our ongoing quest to understand our place in the universe.

Section of the *Epic of Gilgamesh*—Wikipedia

Preservation and conservation challenges

The preservation of Sumerian tablets has been a challenging task for archaeologists and conservators. Many were discovered in archaeological excavations in less than ideal conditions, having been buried for millennia [12]. In recent years, digital preservation has become increasingly important in the field of Sumerian studies [13]. This involves:

- <u>3D scanning</u>: Creating high-resolution digital models of tablets, allowing for detailed study without handling the originals.
- <u>Photogrammetry</u>: Using multiple photographs to create accurate 3D representations of tablets.
- <u>Digital databases</u>: Developing comprehensive online repositories of tablet images and translations, making them accessible to scholars worldwide.
- <u>Machine learning</u>: Applying AI techniques to assist in deciphering damaged or partially legible texts.
- <u>Virtual reality</u>: Creating immersive experiences that allow researchers and the public to interact with virtual representations of the tablets.

These digital preservation efforts serve multiple purposes. They create a permanent record of the tablets in their current state, aid in their study and interpretation, and make the information they contain more widely accessible. Additionally, in cases where the physical tablets continue to degrade despite conservation efforts, these digital records ensure that the information they contain is not lost.

The field of Sumerian tablet preservation continues to evolve, with new technologies and techniques being developed to better understand and protect these invaluable historical artifacts. The combination of traditional conservation methods and cutting-edge digital technologies offers the best hope for preserving this crucial link to our ancient past for future generations.

Societal impact of writing in Sumerian culture

The development of writing had a profound impact on Sumerian society. It allowed for more complex social organization, facilitated long-distance trade, and enabled the preservation and transmission of knowledge across generations [14-15].

The role of scribes and literacy

Sumerian scribes held a prestigious position in society. They underwent extensive training, often starting at a young age, to master the complex cuneiform script [16]. Interestingly, the use of writing was not limited to the elite in Sumerian society. Archaeological evidence suggests that literacy was relatively widespread, with even some women and slaves being able to read and write [17].

Challenges in translation and interpretation

Despite the extensive corpus of Sumerian texts, a significant portion remains untranslated or only partially understood. Estimates suggest that up to 90% of excavated Sumerian tablets have not been fully translated and published [18-19].

The role of artificial intelligence (AI) in Sumerian studies

In recent years, artificial intelligence (AI) has begun to play a role in the translation and analysis of Sumerian texts. Several projects are currently underway to apply AI techniques to cuneiform translation, potentially revolutionizing the field of Sumerian studies [21-23]. These projects involve:

- <u>Automated translation of tablets</u>: AI algorithms, particularly those based on machine learning and neural networks, are being developed to assist in the translation of Sumerian tablets. These systems are trained on existing translations of tablets and can learn to recognize patterns in the cuneiform script. As they improve, they may be able to provide initial translations of newly discovered tablets, which can then be refined by human experts.
- <u>Cuneiform character recognition</u>: One of the biggest challenges in working with Sumerian tablets is accurately identifying individual cuneiform signs, which can vary in appearance due to factors like the scribe's handwriting, damage to the tablet, or erosion over time. AI-powered image recognition systems are being trained to identify these signs more accurately and consistently than human eyes alone, potentially speeding up the process of tablet translation.
- <u>Reconstruction of damaged tablets</u>: AI can be used to help reconstruct damaged or partial tablets. By analyzing patterns in known tablets, AI systems can make educated guesses about missing or illegible parts of a tablet. This could be particularly valuable for

tablets that are fragmentary or poorly preserved.

- <u>Pattern recognition and analysis of tablet collections</u>: AI excels at recognizing patterns in large datasets. In the study of Sumerian tablets, this could be used to identify recurring phrases, grammatical structures, or thematic elements across multiple tablets. This kind of analysis could reveal new insights into Sumerian language, literature, and culture as represented on these clay documents.
- <u>Tablet database management and search</u>: AI can help manage and search the vast databases of digitized Sumerian tablets. Advanced search algorithms can help scholars find relevant tablets or passages more quickly and efficiently than traditional methods.
- <u>Interdisciplinary connections</u>: AI systems can be used to cross-reference Sumerian tablets with other ancient Middle Eastern texts and artifacts, potentially revealing new connections and insights.
- <u>Predictive modeling for tablet discovery</u>: By analyzing patterns in known tablets, AI could potentially predict the likely content of undiscovered tablets, helping to guide archaeological efforts or fill in gaps in our understanding of Sumerian literature and history as recorded on these clay documents.

However, it's important to note that while AI offers exciting possibilities for the study of Sumerian tablets, it is not intended to replace human scholars. Rather, it serves as a powerful tool to augment and accelerate human research on these ancient artifacts. The nuanced understanding of language, culture, and context that human experts bring to the interpretation of Sumerian tablets remains crucial.

Future prospects and potential applications of AI

The potential for further use of AI in Sumerian translation is significant and multifaceted. Optical Character Recognition (OCR) systems could be developed to automatically read and digitize cuneiform signs from photographs or scans of tablets [24]. Machine learning algorithms could be trained to recognize patterns in Sumerian grammar and vocabulary, potentially uncovering new insights into the language's structure [25].

Natural Language Processing (NLP) techniques could be applied to analyze large corpora of Sumerian texts, identifying recurring themes, phrases, or grammatical constructions [26]. AI could also assist in the reconstruction of damaged or fragmentary texts [27].

However, it's important to note that while AI holds great promise for Sumerian studies, it is not a replacement for human expertise.

Ethical considerations and future directions

The application of AI to Sumerian studies also raises important questions about the ethics and methodology of digital humanities. How do we ensure that AI-assisted translations are accurate and culturally sensitive? How might the use of AI change our approach to studying ancient languages and cultures? These are questions that scholars in the field will need to grapple with as AI becomes more prevalent in their work.

Looking to the future, the combination of traditional scholarly methods and cutting-edge AI technologies holds immense promise for unlocking the secrets of Sumerian language and culture. As more texts are translated and analyzed, our understanding of this ancient civilization continues to grow and evolve.

Conclusion

The study of Sumerian language and script is not merely an academic exercise; it provides valuable insights into the origins of human civilization, the development of writing systems, and the complex interplay between language, culture, and society. As we continue to decipher, translate and interpret Sumerian texts, we gain a deeper appreciation for the achievements of this ancient civilization and its lasting impact on human history.

From its unique grammatical structures to its pioneering role in the development of writing, Sumerian continues to fascinate linguists, historians, and archaeologists. The ongoing efforts to translate and understand Sumerian texts, aided by both traditional scholarship and innovative technologies, ensure that this ancient language will continue to reveal its secrets for generations to come.

As we move forward in our exploration of ancient languages and texts, the study of Sumerian serves as a powerful reminder of the enduring human drive to communicate, to record, and to understand our world. In the wedge-shaped impressions on cuneiform tablets, we find not just the words of an ancient people, but a reflection of our own quest for knowledge and meaning.

<u>References</u>

[1] Kramer, S. N. (2010). *The Sumerians: Their History, Culture, and Character*. University of Chicago Press.

[2] Michalowski, P. (2004). Sumerian. *The Cambridge Encyclopedia of the World's Ancient Languages*, edited by R. D. Woodard, Cambridge University Press, pp. 19-59.

[3] Schmandt-Besserat, D. (2022). *Before Writing: From Counting to Cuneiform*. Vol.1. University of Texas Press.

[4] Van De Mieroop, M. (2015). *A History of the Ancient Near East: ca. 3000-323 BCE*. [3rd ed.]. Wiley-Blackwell.

[5] Black, J., & Green, A. (1998). *Gods, Demons and Symbols of Ancient Mesopotamia: An Illustrated Dictionary*. British Museum Press.

[6] Hayes, J. L. (2000). *A Manual of Sumerian Grammar and Texts*. Undena Publications.

[7] Rubio, G. (2007). *Sumerian Morphology. Morphologies of Asia and Africa*, edited by A. S. Kaye, Eisenbrauns, Chapter 46, pp. 1327-1379.

[8] Robson, E. (2007). *Mesopotamian Mathematics. The Mathematics of Egypt, Mesopotamia, China, India, and Islam: A Sourcebook*, edited by V. Katz, Princeton University Press, pp. 57-186.

[9] Englund, Robert K. (1998). Texts from the Late Uruk Period. In Bauer, Joseph; Englund, Robert K.; Krebernik, Manfred (eds.). *Mesopotamien: Späturuk-Zeit und Frühdynastische Zeit*. Orbis Biblicus et Orientalis. Fribourg

et Göttingen: Universitätsverlag Freiburg Schweiz and Vandenhoeck and Ruprecht. pp. 15–233.

[10] Veldhuis, N. (2014). *History of the Cuneiform Lexical Tradition*. Ugarit-Verlag.

[11] George, A. R. (2003). *The Babylonian Gilgamesh Epic: Introduction, Critical Edition and Cuneiform Texts*. Oxford University Press.

[12] Pedersén, O. (1998). *Archives and Libraries in the Ancient Near East, 1500-300 B.C.* CDL Press.

[13] *Digitalised Cuneiform*. (2021). Cuneiform Digital Library Initiative. <https://cdli.ucla.edu/ >

[14] Charpin, D. (2010). *Reading and Writing in Babylon*. Harvard University Press.

15] Postgate, J. N. (2017). *Early Mesopotamia: Society and Economy at the Dawn of History*. Routledge.

[16] Tinney, S. (1998). Texts, Tablets, and Teaching: Scribal Education in Nippur and Ur. *Expedition: The magazine of the University of Pennsylvania*, vol. 40, no. 2, pp. 40-50.

[17] Charpin, D. (2010). *Writing, Law, and Kingship in Old Babylonian Mesopotamia*. University of Chicago Press.

[18] Veldhuis, N. (2012). Cuneiform: Changes and Developments. In *The Shape of Script: How and Why Writing Systems Change*, edited by S. D. Houston, School for Advanced Research Press, pp. 3-23.

[19] Civil, M. (1995). Ancient Mesopotamian Lexicography. *Civilizations of the Ancient Near East*, edited by J. M. Sasson, Scribner, pp. 2305-2314.

[20] Steinkeller, P. (2002). Archaic City Seals and the Question of Early Babylonian Unity. *Assyria and Beyond: Studies Presented to Mogens Trolle Larsen*, edited by J. G. Dercksen, Eisenbrauns. pp. 249-257.

[21] Pagé-Perron, É., et al. (2017). Machine Translation and Automated Analysis of the Sumerian Language. *Proceedings of the Joint SIGHUM Workshop on Computational Linguistics for Cultural Heritage, Social Sciences, Humanities and Literature,* pp. 10-16.

[22] Jauhiainen, H., et al. (2019). Cuneiform OCR via Deep Learning. *Proceedings of the 15th International Conference on Document Analysis and Recognition,* pp. 642-647.

[23] Gordin, S., et al. (2020). Babylonian Engine: A Deep NLP and Digital Humanities Instrument for Babylonian Scholarly Texts. *Proceedings of the 12th Language Resources and Evaluation Conference,* pp. 2613-2621.

[24] Mara, H., et al. (2010). GigaMesh and Gilgamesh: 3D Multiscale Integral Invariant Cuneiform Character Extraction. *Proceedings of the 11th International Symposium on Virtual Reality, Archaeology and Cultural Heritage,* pp. 131-138.

[25] Homburg, T., & Chiarcos, C. (2016). Akkadian Word Segmentation. *Proceedings of the 10th International Conference on Language Resources and Evaluation,* pp. 4067-4074.

[26] Liu, C., et al. (2015). Unsupervised Alignment of Sumerian-Akkadian Parallel Texts. *Proceedings of the 2015 Conference of the North American Chapter of the Association for Computational Linguistics: Human Language Technologies,* pp. 1460-1465.

[27] Fetaya, E., et al. (2020). Restoration of fragmentary Babylonian texts using recurrent neural networks. *Proceedings of the National Academy of Sciences,* 117(37), pp. 22743-22751.

◉

CHAPTER THREE

Egyptian hieroglyphs and Demotic script

The ancient Egyptians wrote on everything from stone to leather, on artifacts of every shape and size, and in characters that are as beautiful as they are arcane.

Barbara Mertz, 'Red Land, Black Land: Daily Life in Ancient Egypt'. [1]

The ancient Egyptian writing systems, particularly hieroglyphs and Demotic script, stand as enduring testaments to one of the world's oldest and most fascinating civilizations. These scripts not only served as a means of communication but also as intricate art forms and repositories of cultural knowledge. This chapter delves into the rich history, unique features, and contemporary relevance of these writing systems, exploring their use, preservation, and the cutting-edge technologies being employed to unlock their remaining secrets.

Origins and historical context

The development of writing in ancient Egypt is a story that spans millennia, beginning with the emergence of hieroglyphs around 3200 BCE [2]. Hieroglyphs, derived from the Greek words 'hieros' (sacred) and 'glyphos' (carved), were initially used for monumental inscriptions and religious texts. This elaborate script, with its intricate pictorial symbols, would continue to be used for over 3,500 years, making it one of the longest-used writing systems in human history [3].

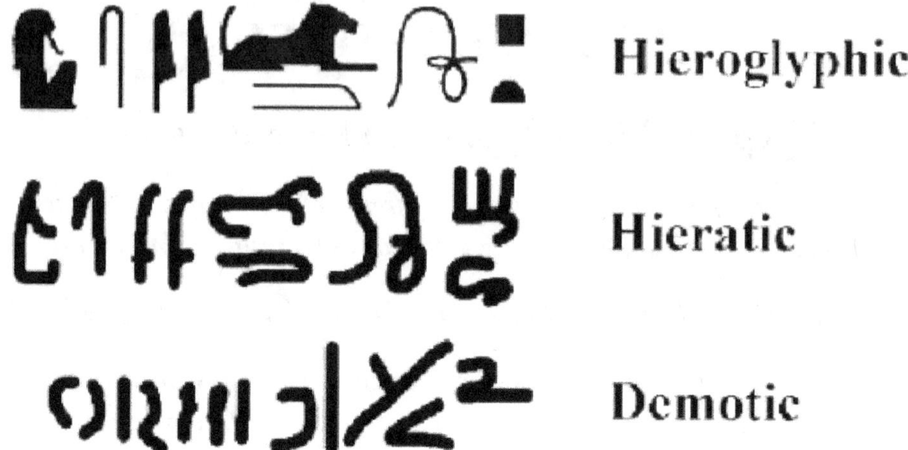

As Egyptian society evolved, so did its writing systems. The hieratic script, a cursive form of hieroglyphs, emerged around 2700 BCE as a faster, more practical writing method for everyday use [4]. Later, around 650 BCE, the Demotic script developed as an even more simplified and rapid writing system, used primarily for administrative, legal, and commercial documents [5].

Geographical distribution and evolution

The use of Egyptian scripts was primarily concentrated in the Nile Valley and Delta, the heartland of ancient Egyptian civilization. However, as Egypt's influence spread, so did its writing systems. Hieroglyphs and their derivatives were used in Nubia to the south, and inscriptions have been found as far afield as the Sinai Peninsula and parts of the Middle East[6].

The evolution of Egyptian scripts reflects the changing political and cultural landscape of ancient Egypt. Hieroglyphs remained the prestigious script for monumental and religious texts throughout Egypt's history, even as hieratic and Demotic became more prevalent for everyday use. The Ptolemaic period (332-30 BCE) saw an increase in the complexity of hieroglyphic writing, possibly as a reaction to the growing influence of Greek culture [7].

Linguistic features and complexities

Egyptian hieroglyphs represent one of the most complex writing systems ever devised. The script consists of over 1,000 distinct characters, including ideograms (representing ideas), phonograms (representing sounds), and determinatives (clarifying the meaning of other signs) [8]. This complexity allowed for great precision in expression but also made the system challenging to learn and use.

One of the most intriguing aspects of hieroglyphic writing is its flexibility. A single hieroglyph could function as an ideogram, a phonogram, or a determinative, depending on context. This multivalent nature of signs allowed for creative wordplay and layered meanings, particularly in religious and literary texts [9].

The Demotic script, while simpler in appearance, retained much of the underlying structure of hieroglyphic writing. It used a smaller set of characters, many of which were ligatures or simplified forms of hieroglyphs. Despite its cursive nature, Demotic still incorporated ideograms and determinatives, maintaining a connection to its hieroglyphic roots [10].

Decipherment and translation challenges

The decipherment of Egyptian hieroglyphs is one of the great intellectual achievements of the 19th century. The process began with the discovery of the *Rosetta Stone* in 1799, which provided parallel texts in hieroglyphs, Demotic, and Greek [11]. Jean-François Champollion's breakthrough in 1822, recognizing that hieroglyphs represented both ideographic and phonetic elements, laid the foundation for modern Egyptology [12].

Before the *Rosetta Stone*, hieroglyphs were seen as little more than decorative symbols, their meaning lost to time. However, by comparing the Greek inscription to the hieroglyphic and Demotic ones, scholars were able to identify specific hieroglyphs with corresponding Greek words, gradually unraveling the ancient Egyptian language.

The *Rosetta Stone's* impact on our understanding of Egyptian civilization is profound. It opened a window into the past, allowing us to read and interpret ancient Egyptian texts, including literature, religious documents, and historical records. This newfound knowledge has revealed much about the Egyptians' beliefs, customs, and achievements, shedding light on their complex society and rich culture. Furthermore, the ability to decipher hieroglyphs has enabled archaeologists to better understand the context of their discoveries, providing valuable insights into the daily lives, rituals, and technological advancements of the ancient Egyptians.

Despite this breakthrough, challenges in translation persist. The vast time span over which Egyptian was written means that the language underwent significant changes. Old Egyptian, Middle Egyptian, Late Egyptian, and Coptic represent distinct phases in the language's evolution, each with its own grammatical and lexical peculiarities [13]. Additionally, many texts contain specialized vocabulary related to religion, administration, or specific professions, requiring deep contextual knowledge for accurate translation.

Rosetta Stone — British Museum

The Egyptian textual corpus

The corpus of ancient Egyptian texts is vast and diverse, spanning over three millennia of continuous use. It includes:

- Monumental inscriptions on temples, tombs, and stelae
- Religious texts such as the *Pyramid Texts*, *Coffin Texts*, and *Book of the Dead*
- Literary works including poetry, stories, and wisdom texts
- Administrative and legal documents
- Scientific and medical texts
- Personal letters and graffiti.

The total number of known Egyptian texts is difficult to quantify precisely, but it is estimated to be in the hundreds of thousands [14]. These texts are scattered across museums, libraries, and archaeological sites worldwide, with major collections housed in institutions such as the Egyptian Museum in Cairo, the British Museum in London, and the Louvre in Paris [15].

Preservation and conservation

The preservation of Egyptian texts has been aided by Egypt's arid climate, which has allowed many papyri and inscriptions to survive for millennia. However, conservation remains a critical concern. Stone inscriptions face threats from environmental factors and human activity, while papyri are particularly vulnerable to degradation [16].

Modern conservation efforts employ a range of techniques, from climate-controlled storage for papyri to 3D scanning of monumental inscriptions. Digital preservation has become increasingly important, with projects like the Thesaurus Linguae Aegyptiae creating comprehensive digital corpora of Egyptian texts [17].

Societal impact of writing in ancient Egyptian culture

Writing played a central role in ancient Egyptian society, permeating nearly every aspect of life. In the religious sphere, hieroglyphs were considered sacred, capable of bringing into being the realities they described. This belief in the power of writing is evident in practices such as the ritualistic 'opening of the mouth' ceremony performed on statues and mummies, which involved touching the mouth with hieroglyphic signs to animate the deceased [18].

In the administrative realm, writing was crucial for the functioning of the centralized Egyptian state. Records of harvests, tax collection, and legal proceedings were meticulously kept, often in hieratic or Demotic script. The ability to write was a key to social advancement, with scribes holding prestigious positions in the bureaucracy [19].

Egyptian writing also served important cultural functions. Literary texts, including stories, poems, and wisdom literature, were composed and copied, contributing to a rich intellectual tradition. The 'Houses of Life', associated with temples, acted as centers of learning and scriptoria, where religious and scientific texts were studied and reproduced [20].

The role of scribes and literacy

Scribes occupied a privileged position in ancient Egyptian society. The training to become a scribe was rigorous, typically beginning in childhood and lasting several years. Scribal education involved not only learning the complex writing systems but also acquiring knowledge of mathematics, administration, and religious texts [21].

While literacy rates in ancient Egypt were low by modern standards, they were relatively high for an ancient civilization. It's estimated that in some periods, up to 5-10% of the population may have had some degree of literacy [22]. This included not only professional scribes but also administrators, priests, and some craftsmen.

The prestige associated with writing is reflected in Egyptian art, where scribes are often depicted with the tools of their trade – ink wells, reed brushes, and papyrus sheets. The god Thoth, patron of scribes, was one of the most important deities in the Egyptian pantheon, further underscoring the cultural significance of writing [23].

Ancient Egyptian Scribe— AI depiction: Gillam

Untranslated corpus and ongoing challenges

Despite centuries of study, a significant portion of the Egyptian textual corpus remains untranslated or only partially understood. This is due to several factors:

- The sheer volume of texts, with new discoveries continually being made
- The specialized nature of many texts, requiring deep contextual knowledge
- Damage to texts, leaving gaps in our understanding
- The evolving nature of the Egyptian language over its long history.

It's difficult to quantify precisely how much of the corpus is untranslated, but estimates suggest that significant portions of administrative and economic texts, as well as many fragmentary literary and religious works, await full translation and analysis [24].

One of the most challenging areas is the corpus of medical texts. While some, like the *Edwin Smith Papyrus*, have been extensively studied, many others contain specialized vocabulary and concepts that are still not fully understood [25]. Similarly, many technical texts relating to topics such as astronomy, mathematics, and ritual practices present ongoing challenges to translators.

Egyptian hieroglyphics — Wordpress

Application of AI to Egyptian texts

In recent years, artificial intelligence (AI) has begun to play an increasingly important role in the study of ancient Egyptian texts. Several projects are currently applying AI techniques to various aspects of Egyptology, including text recognition, translation, and analysis.

One notable project is the 'Machine Learning and Ancient Languages' initiative at the University of California, Los Angeles. This project is developing AI algorithms to assist in the reading and translation of Demotic texts, which are particularly challenging due to their cursive nature [26]. The algorithms are being trained on a corpus of known texts to recognize patterns and assist in deciphering damaged or unclear passages.

Another significant effort is the Rosetta Stone Project, a collaboration between computer scientists and Egyptologists at several institutions. This project aims to create a comprehensive digital corpus of Egyptian texts, using AI to assist in text recognition, categorization, and cross-referencing [27].

The Bonn University in Germany is leading a project called 'Analiticš Hieroglyphica', which uses machine learning techniques to analyze the structure and evolution of hieroglyphic signs over time. This could provide new insights into the development of the writing system and aid in the dating and categorization of texts [28]. The project, launched in 2014, has been dedicated to creating a comprehensive digital database of Maya inscriptions. This includes cataloging thousands of hieroglyphic characters, many of which are variants of the same word, making the script particularly complex to decipher. The project also aims to construct a dictionary of Classic Maya, integrating digital tools that automate the transcription, transliteration, and translation of hieroglyphic texts. It is supplemented by an image database with over 40,000 photos of inscriptions on archaeological sites and objects, helping scholars make progress on previously undecipherable texts.

Potential for further AI applications

The potential for further use of AI in the study of Egyptian texts is vast and multifaceted. Some promising areas include:

- <u>Optical Character Recognition (OCR) for hieroglyphs and Demotic</u>: Advanced OCR systems could greatly accelerate the process of digitizing and cataloging Egyptian texts. While challenges remain due to the complexity and variability of the scripts, progress in this area could revolutionize access to the textual corpus [29].

- <u>Machine translation</u>: While fully automated translation of ancient Egyptian is still a distant goal, AI could assist human translators by suggesting possible readings for unclear passages or identifying parallel phrases in known texts [30].
- <u>Pattern recognition and stylistic analysis</u>: AI algorithms could be used to identify patterns in vocabulary, grammar, and style across large corpora of texts. This could aid in attribution, dating, and understanding the evolution of literary and religious traditions [31].
- <u>Reconstruction of damaged texts</u>: Machine learning models, trained on intact texts, could potentially assist in reconstructing damaged or fragmentary inscriptions and papyri [32].
- <u>Cross-linguistic analysis</u>: AI could help in comparing Egyptian texts with those of contemporary civilizations, potentially uncovering new connections and influences [33].
- <u>3D modeling and virtual reconstruction</u>: AI-assisted 3D scanning and modeling could help in preserving and studying monumental inscriptions, allowing for detailed analysis without risking damage to the original artifacts [34].

Challenges and ethical considerations

While the potential of AI in Egyptology is exciting, it also presents challenges and ethical considerations. There's a risk of over-reliance on automated systems, potentially leading to misinterpretations if not carefully checked by human experts. Additionally, as AI systems become more prevalent, there's a need to ensure that traditional philological skills are not lost [35].

There are also important questions about data ownership and access. As digital corpora are created and AI models are trained on them, who owns the resulting data and algorithms? How can equitable access be ensured for scholars worldwide, particularly those in Egypt and other countries with significant Egyptian heritage? [36]

Furthermore, the application of AI to ancient texts raises philosophical questions about the nature of language and meaning. Can a machine truly understand the nuances and cultural contexts embedded in ancient Egyptian writing, or will there always be aspects that require human interpretation? [37]

Future directions and interdisciplinary approaches

The future of Egyptian textual studies likely lies in interdisciplinary approaches that combine traditional philological methods with cutting-edge technology. Collaborations between Egyptologists, computer scientists, linguists, and experts in other relevant fields will be crucial in developing effective and responsible AI applications [38].

One promising direction is the integration of AI with other scientific techniques used in archaeology and conservation. For example, AI could be combined with spectral imaging techniques to read previously invisible text on papyri or palimpsests [39]. Similarly, AI could assist in analyzing the chemical composition of inks and pigments, providing new insights into scribal practices and text production [40].

Another important area for future research is the development of AI systems that can work across multiple ancient languages and scripts. Many Egyptian texts, particularly from later periods, contain influences from or direct translations into other languages such as Greek, Aramaic, or Coptic. AI systems that can navigate these multilingual environments could provide new insights into cultural interactions and the transmission of knowledge in the ancient world [41].

Conclusion

The study of Egyptian hieroglyphs and Demotic script continues to yield fascinating insights into one of the world's most enduring civilizations. From monumental inscriptions that have stood for millennia to fragile papyri preserving the thoughts and deeds of ancient Egyptians, these texts offer a window into a rich and complex culture.

As we move forward, the integration of traditional scholarly methods with advanced technologies like AI promises to open new frontiers in our understanding of ancient Egypt. However, it's crucial that this progress is balanced with a deep respect for the cultural significance of these texts and a commitment to ethical and inclusive research practices.

The decipherment of hieroglyphs in the 19th century revolutionized our understanding of Ancient Egypt. Perhaps the application of AI in the 21st century will lead to equally transformative discoveries, unlocking secrets that have remained hidden for thousands of years. As we continue to explore these ancient writings, we not only learn about Egypt's past but also gain insights into the fundamental human drive to communicate, to record, and to understand our world.

In the end, the study of Egyptian scripts is not merely an academic exercise. It's a journey into the hearts and minds of people who lived thousands of years ago, yet whose hopes, fears, and aspirations continue to resonate with us today. As we employ new tools to unlock the secrets of these ancient texts, we honor the scribes who meticulously recorded their world, keeping their legacy alive for future generations to discover and appreciate.

<u>References</u>

[1] Mertz, B. (2008). *Red Land, Black Land: Daily Life in Ancient Egypt.* William Morrow Paperbacks.

[2] Allen, J. P. (2014). *Middle Egyptian: An Introduction to the Language and Culture of Hieroglyphs.* [3rd ed.]. Cambridge University Press.

[3] Loprieno, A. (1997). *Ancient Egyptian: A Linguistic Introduction.* Diachronica, *14*(2), 373-378.

[4] Parkinson, R., & Quirke, S. (1995). *Papyrus.* University of Texas Press. [Egyptian Bookshelf].

[5] Johnson, J. H. (1991). *Thus Wrote 'Onchsheshonqy': An Introductory Grammar of Demotic.* Oriental Institute of the University of Chicago.

[6] O'Connor, D. (1993). *Ancient Nubia: Egypt's Rival in Africa.* University of Pennsylvania Museum of Archaeology and Anthropology.

[7] Andrews, C. (1994). *Amulets of Ancient Egypt*. British Museum Press.

[8] Gardiner, A. (1957). *Egyptian Grammar: Being an Introduction to the Study of Hieroglyphs*. [3rd ed. revised.]. Griffith Institute Publications.

[9] Goldwasser, O. (1995). *From Icon to Metaphor: Studies in the Semiotics of the Hieroglyphs*. Vol. 142. Friborg University Press.

[10] Depauw, M. (1997). *A Companion to Demotic Studies*. Brussels, Fondation Égyptologique Reine Élisabeth.

[11] Parkinson, R. (2005). *The Rosetta Stone*. British Museum Press.

[12] Robinson, A. (2013). *Cracking the Egyptian Code: The Revolutionary Life of Jean-François Champollion*. Thames & Hudson.

[13] Junge, F. (2001). *Late Egyptian Grammar: An Introduction*. Griffith Institute.

[14] Lesko, L. H. (1994). *Pharaoh's Workers: The Villagers of Deir el Medina*. Cornell University Press.

[15] Quirke, S. (2010). *Hidden Hands: Egyptian Workforces in Petrie Excavation Archives, 1880–1924*. Duckworth.

[16] Nicholson, P. T., & Shaw, I. (Eds.). (2000). *Ancient Egyptian Materials and Technology*. Cambridge University Press.

[17] Studwick, N. (2005). *Texts from the Pyramid Age*. Vol. 16. Brill.

[18] Assmann, J. (2011). *Death and Salvation in Ancient Egypt*. Cornell University Press.

[19] Kemp, B. J. (2006). *Ancient Egypt: Anatomy of a Civilization*. Routledge.

[20] Baines, J. (2007). *Visual and Written Culture in Ancient Egypt*. Oxford University Press.

[21] Wente, E. F. (1990). *Letters from Ancient Egypt*. Scholars Press.

[22] Baines, J., & Eyre, C. J. (1983). Four Notes on Literacy. Göttinger Miszellen, 61, 65-96. Reprinted in J. Baines, *Visual and Written Culture in Ancient Egypt*, Oxford University Press, 2007, 63-94.

[23] Bleeker, C. J. (1973). *Hathor and Thoth: Two Key Figures of the Ancient Egyptian Religion* (pp. 158-160). Brill.

[24] Redford, D. B. (Ed.). (2002). *The Oxford Encyclopedia of Ancient Egypt*. Oxford University Press.

[25] Nunn, J. F. (2002). *Ancient Egyptian Medicine*. University of Oklahoma Press.

[26] Mara, H., Krömker, S., Jakob, S., & Breuckmann, B. (2010). GigaMesh and Gilgamesh - 3D Multiscale Integral Invariant Cuneiform Character Extraction. In A. Artusi et al. (Eds.), *VAST'10, Proceedings of the 11th International Conference on Virtual Reality, Archaeology and Cultural Heritage* (pp. 131-138).

[27] Rosmorduc, S. (2015). Computational Linguistics in Egyptology. In Julie Stauder-Porchet, et al., (Eds.). *UCLA Encyclopedia of Egyptology*, Los Angeles.

[28] Hafemann, I., Huber, B., Nederhof, M., Rodrigues, F., & Sojic, A. (2018). A Digital Corpus of Egyptian Hieroglyphic Texts. In S. Polis (Ed.), *Proceedings of the 5th Egyptological Tempeltagung* (pp. 123-134). Harrassowitz Verlag.

[29] Franken, M., & van Gemert, J. (2013). Automatic Egyptian Hieroglyph Recognition by Retrieving Images as Texts. In *Proceedings of the 21st ACM International Conference on Multimedia* (pp. 765-768).

[30] Nederhof, M. J. & Berti, M. (2015). OCR of Handwritten Transcriptions of Ancient Egyptian Hieroglyphic Text. In S. Polis & J. Winand (Eds.), *Texts, Languages & Information Technology in Egyptology* (pp. 123-134). Presses Universitaires de Liège.

[31] Goler, S., Yardley, J. T., Cacciola, A., Hagadorn, A., Ratzan, D., & Botto, R. (2016). Characterizing the Age of Ancient Egyptian Manuscripts through

Micro-Raman Spectroscopy. *Journal of Raman Spectroscopy*, 47(10), 1185-1193.

[32] Hamed, M. M., & Abdelrahman, O. H. (2019). Machine Learning in Restoring Fragmented Ancient Egyptian Texts. *International Journal of Advanced Computer Science and Applications*, 10(6), 129-134.

[33] Dirksen, V., & von Hagen, J. (2019). Exploring Ancient Egyptian Texts with AI: A Case Study. In *Proceedings of the 2nd International Conference on Digital Heritage* (pp. 145-150).

[34] Stanco, F., Battiato, S., & Gallo, G. (Eds.). (2011). *Digital Imaging for Cultural Heritage Preservation: Analysis, Restoration, and Reconstruction of Ancient Artworks*. CRC Press.

[35] Manovich, L. (2015). Data Science and Digital Art History. *International Journal for Digital Art History*, 1, 12-35.

[36] Manžuch, Z. (2017). Ethical issues in digitization of cultural heritage. *Journal of Contemporary Archival Studies*, 4(2), 4.

[37] Searle, J. R. (1980). Minds, Brains, and Programs. *Behavioral and Brain Sciences*, 3(3), 417-424.

[38] Terras, M. (2016). The Digital Classicist: Disciplinary Focus and Interdisciplinary Vision. In G. Bodard & S. Mahony (Eds.), *Digital Research in the Study of Classical Antiquity* (pp. 171-189). Routledge.

[39] Bearman, G., & Spiro, S. (1996). Archaeological Applications of Advanced Imaging Techniques. *Biblical Archaeologist*, 59(1), 56-66.

[40] Hahn, O., Weinberg, G., Rabin, I., Wolff, T., & Masic, A. (2009). On the Origin of the Ink of the Thanksgiving Scroll (1QHodayota). *Dead Sea Discoveries*, 16(1), 97-106.

[41] Schubert, P. (2009). Editing a Bilingual Text: The Coptic-Greek Psalter as a Case-Study. In D. Buzzetti & J. McGann (Eds.), *Electronic Textual Editing* (pp. 45-56). Modern Language Association of America.

TRANSLATING ANCIENT TEXTS

53

CHAPTER FOUR

Akkadian

Akkadian was the language of diplomacy for the entire ancient Near East, from Greece to Iran and from the Black Sea to the southern tip of the Arabian Peninsula.

John Huehnergard, 'A Grammar of Akkadian', 2011. [1]

Akkadian stands as a testament to one of the world's earliest and most influential civilizations. As the lingua franca of the ancient Middle East for more than two millennia, Akkadian played a crucial role in shaping the cultural, political, and economic landscape of the region. This chapter invites you to explore the fascinating world of Akkadian studies, where cutting-edge technologies and passionate scholarship are revolutionizing our understanding of this ancient language and the civilization it represents [1].

Ancient Akkadian was primarily written using the cuneiform script, which was developed in ancient Mesopotamia. Cuneiform, meaning 'wedge-shaped', was created by pressing a reed stylus into soft clay tablets, resulting in distinctive wedge-like impressions. This script was originally developed for writing Sumerian but was later adapted for Akkadian and other languages of the region.

The Akkadian version of cuneiform evolved over time, becoming more syllabic in nature compared to its Sumerian predecessor. It incorporated both logographic (word-signs) and syllabic elements, with hundreds of signs representing syllables, words, and determinatives (signs that indicated the category of the following word). The complexity of the script meant that literacy was largely confined to scribes who underwent years of training to master it. Cuneiform was used to write Akkadian from around the 24th century BCE until its gradual replacement by alphabetic scripts in the first millennium BCE.

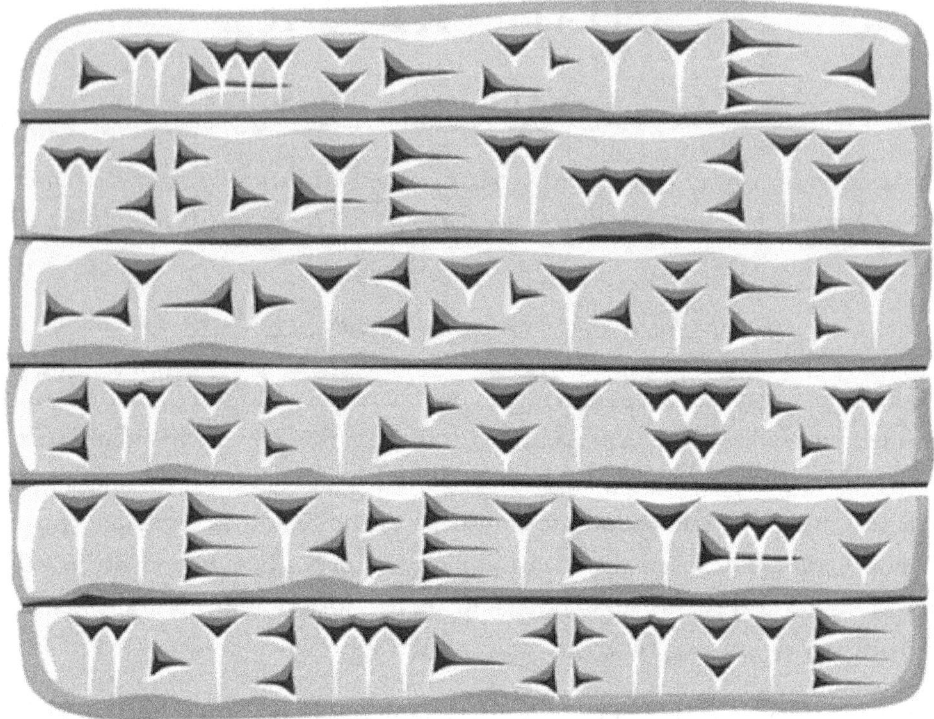

Akkadian cuneiform. Freepik: valadzionak_volha

Origins and historical context

Around 2800 BCE, Akkadian emerged in what is now modern-day Iraq [2]. Named after the city of Akkad, it belonged to the Semitic language family and gradually replaced Sumerian as the dominant language of the region. Akkadian's use spanned over two millennia, from the 3rd millennium BCE to the 1st century CE, making it one of the longest-used languages in human history [3].

Akkadian evolved through several stages:

- Old Akkadian (2500-1950 BCE)
- Old Babylonian and Old Assyrian (1950-1530 BCE)
- Middle Babylonian and Middle Assyrian (1530-1000 BCE)
- Neo-Babylonian and Neo-Assyrian (1000-600 BCE)

- Late Babylonian (600 BCE – 100 CE) [4].

Each period saw shifts in grammar, vocabulary, and usage, reflecting the changing political and cultural landscapes of Mesopotamia. It's like watching a language breathe and grow over thousands of years, adapting to the needs of its speakers and the world around them. During the Late Babylonian period, Akkadian was gradually replaced by Aramaic as the common language of Mesopotamia.

Geographical distribution and evolution

From its Mesopotamian homeland, Akkadian's influence extended to the Mediterranean coast, the Persian Gulf, Anatolia, and Egypt [5]. This wasn't just a language; it was a cultural bridge, facilitating trade, diplomacy, and the exchange of ideas across an area larger than many modern nations.

The language's evolution was closely tied to the political fortunes of Mesopotamian empires. Picture the grandeur of the Neo-Assyrian period when Akkadian reached its widest geographical spread [6]. Even after its decline as a spoken language, Akkadian continued to be used in scholarly and religious contexts well into the Hellenistic period.

Linguistic features and complexities

Akkadian has some unique features with the script using a combination of logographic (word) signs and syllabic signs [7].

Akkadian's verbal system was intricate and expressive. Like a machine with many parts, Akkadian verbs used different stems to convey various shades of meaning [8]. This allowed for precise communication of actions and states in ways that continue to interest scholars today.

Another interesting feature of Akkadian was its use of the subjunctive mood, shown by the suffix -am/-nim. This suffix could indicate movement towards the speaker, but also expressed purpose or intent [9]. These layers of meaning make Akkadian a rich subject for study and interpretation.

The Akkadian textual corpus

The corpus of Akkadian texts is incredibly diverse, including:

- Royal inscriptions and annals
- Legal and administrative documents
- Literary works, including epics, myths, and wisdom literature
- Scientific and medical texts
- Personal and official letters
- Religious and divinatory texts.

The sheer volume of this corpus is staggering. Estimates suggest there are hundreds of thousands of known Akkadian texts, with new discoveries continually adding to this number [10]. These texts are scattered across museums, universities, and archaeological sites worldwide, with major collections housed in institutions such as the British Museum, the Louvre, and the Iraq Museum in Baghdad [11].

Preservation and conservation

The preservation of these ancient voices is a crucial and ongoing task. While the durability of clay tablets has aided in the survival of many texts, time has taken its toll. Many tablets have been damaged or fragmented, posing significant challenges for translation and interpretation.

Modern conservation efforts employ a range of techniques. Conservators carefully clean and stabilize clay tablets for future generations. Meanwhile, in high-tech labs, advanced imaging technologies are revealing previously invisible text, bringing long-lost words back to light [12].

In recent years, digital preservation has become increasingly important. Imagine a vast digital library, accessible from anywhere in the world. Projects like the Cuneiform Digital Library Initiative (CDLI) are working to create comprehensive digital corpora of Akkadian texts, democratizing access to these ancient writings and ensuring their preservation for the digital age [13].

Societal impact of Akkadian

To truly understand Akkadian, we must consider its role in ancient Mesopotamian society. In the administrative sphere, it was the language of record-keeping, legal documents, and royal decrees. The famous *Code of Hammurabi*, one of the earliest known legal codes, was written in Akkadian [14], its laws shaping society and influencing legal traditions for generations to come.

In the religious domain, Akkadian was the language of hymns, prayers, and ritual texts. Many Sumerian religious texts were translated into Akkadian, contributing to the preservation and spread of Mesopotamian religious traditions [15].

Akkadian also served as a language of literature and scholarship. Notably, the *Epic of Gilgamesh* [16]. The narrative follows Gilgamesh's journey from a tyrannical ruler to a wise and humbled hero. Along the way, he befriends the wild man Enkidu, and together they embark on several adventures, defeating powerful monsters and earning divine wrath. After Enkidu's death, Gilgamesh becomes obsessed with his own mortality and seeks immortality. His quest leads him to Utnapishtim, the survivor of a great flood, who teaches him about the futility of seeking eternal life. Ultimately, Gilgamesh returns to Uruk, having gained wisdom and acceptance of his human fate. The epic explores themes of friendship, the human condition, the power of civilization, and the inevitability of death.

This epic tale, along with countless other literary works, was composed and transmitted in Akkadian, forming a rich literary tradition that continues to captivate readers today.

The role of scribes and literacy

At the heart of Akkadian's use and transmission were the scribes, highly trained professionals who held a prestigious position in Mesopotamian society. Young apprentices in 'tablet houses', the scribal schools of ancient Mesopotamia, spending years mastering the complex cuneiform script and the intricacies of the Akkadian language [17].

While exact literacy rates are difficult to determine, it's estimated that in some periods, up to 5% of the urban population may have been literate in Akkadian [18]. This included not only professional scribes but also administrators, priests, and merchants. This was a society where the ability to read and write was a mark of status and power, opening doors to influential positions in government, religion, and commerce.

Untranslated corpus and ongoing challenges

Despite centuries of study, a significant portion of the Akkadian corpus remains untranslated or only partially understood. This is due to several factors:

- The sheer volume of texts, with new discoveries continually being made
- The specialized nature of many texts, requiring deep contextual knowledge
- Damage to tablets, leaving gaps in the text
- The evolving nature of the Akkadian language over its long history.

It's estimated that as much as 90% of the known Akkadian corpus may still await full translation and analysis [19]. This includes large numbers of administrative and economic texts, which, while less glamorous than literary or religious works, can provide valuable insights into daily life in ancient Mesopotamia.

One particularly challenging area is the corpus of medical texts. While some, like the *Diagnostic Handbook*, have been extensively studied, many others contain specialized vocabulary and concepts that are still not fully understood [20]. Imagine the excitement of a scholar deciphering a medical text, potentially uncovering ancient remedies or surgical techniques lost to time.

Application of AI to Akkadian texts

As we look to the future of Akkadian studies, cutting-edge technologies are opening up new possibilities for research and discovery. Artificial intelligence (AI) has begun to play an increasingly important role in the study of Akkadian texts. Several projects are currently applying AI techniques to various aspects of Assyriology, including text recognition, translation, and analysis.

One notable project is the Babylonian Engine initiative led by Shai Gordin at Ariel University in Israel. This project uses natural language processing techniques to analyze Akkadian texts, with the goal of creating tools to assist in translation and interpretation [21]. Imagine an AI system sifting through thousands of tablets, identifying patterns and connections that might take human scholars years to discover.

Another significant effort is the 'Machine Translation and Automated Analysis of Cuneiform Languages' project, a collaboration between several universities. This project aims to develop machine learning algorithms to assist in the reading and translation of cuneiform tablets, including those in Akkadian [22]. Picture a future where AI and human scholars work side-by-side, each complementing the other's strengths in the quest to understand ancient texts.

The Cuneiform Digital Library Initiative (CDLI), based at the University of California, Los Angeles, is also incorporating AI techniques into its work. The CDLI is developing tools to help identify and categorize cuneiform signs, which could greatly accelerate the process of digitizing and translating Akkadian texts [23]. Imagine a vast digital library of Akkadian texts, fully searchable and cross-referenced, opening up new avenues for research and discovery.

Potential for further AI applications

The potential for further use of AI in the study of Akkadian texts is vast and multifaceted. Some promising areas include:

- Optical Character Recognition (OCR) for cuneiform: Advanced OCR systems could greatly accelerate the process of digitizing and cataloging Akkadian texts. While challenges remain due to the complexity of cuneiform script, progress in this area could revolutionize access to the textual corpus [24].
- Machine translation: While fully automated translation of Akkadian is still a distant goal, AI could assist human translators by suggesting

possible readings for unclear passages or identifying parallel phrases in known texts [25].

- <u>Pattern recognition and stylistic analysis</u>: AI algorithms could be used to identify patterns in vocabulary, grammar, and style across large corpora of texts. This could aid in attribution, dating, and understanding the evolution of literary and religious traditions [26].
- <u>Reconstruction of damaged texts</u>: Machine learning models, trained on intact texts, could potentially assist in reconstructing damaged or fragmentary tablets [27]. Imagine an AI system filling in the gaps of a broken tablet, bringing long-lost words back to life.
- <u>Cross-linguistic analysis</u>: AI could help in comparing Akkadian texts with those in related languages, potentially uncovering new connections and influences [28].
- <u>3D modeling and virtual reconstruction</u>: AI-assisted 3D scanning and modeling could help in preserving and studying cuneiform tablets, allowing for detailed analysis without risking damage to the original artifacts [29].

Challenges and ethical considerations

While the potential of AI in the study of Akkadian is exciting, it also presents challenges and ethical considerations. There's a risk of over-reliance on automated systems, potentially leading to misinterpretations if not carefully checked by human experts. Additionally, as AI systems become more prevalent, there's a need to ensure that traditional philological skills are not lost [30].

There are also important questions about data ownership and access. As digital corpora are created and AI models are trained on them, who owns the resulting data and algorithms? How can equitable access be ensured for scholars worldwide, particularly those in countries with significant Mesopotamian heritage? [31]

Furthermore, the application of AI to ancient texts raises philosophical questions about the nature of language and meaning. Can a machine truly understand the nuances and cultural contexts embedded in Akkadian writing, or will there always be aspects that require human interpretation? [32]

Future directions and interdisciplinary approaches

The future of Akkadian studies likely lies in interdisciplinary approaches that combine traditional philological methods with cutting-edge technology. Collaborations between Assyriologists, computer scientists, linguists, and experts in other relevant fields will be crucial in developing effective and responsible AI applications [33].

One promising direction is the integration of AI with other scientific techniques used in archaeology and conservation. For example, AI could be combined with spectral imaging techniques to read previously invisible text on damaged tablets [34]. Similarly, AI could assist in analyzing the chemical composition of clay tablets, providing new insights into their provenance and production methods [35].

Another important area for future research is the development of AI systems that can work across multiple ancient languages and scripts. Many Akkadian texts, particularly from later periods, contain influences from or direct translations into other languages such as Aramaic or Greek. AI systems that can navigate these multilingual environments could provide new insights into cultural interactions and the transmission of knowledge in the ancient world [36].

Virtual reality and immersive experiences

Imagine stepping into the shoes of an ancient Mesopotamian scribe, feeling the clay tablet in your hands as you inscribe cuneiform characters. This is no longer a mere fantasy. Dr. Sarah Chen, a digital archaeologist at Stanford University, is pioneering the use of virtual reality in Akkadian studies.

"We're creating immersive environments where students and researchers can experience ancient Mesopotamia firsthand," Dr. Chen explained. "You can walk through a reconstructed Babylonian temple, read inscriptions on the walls, even participate in scribal training exercises." [37]

These VR experiences are not just educational tools; they're also pushing the boundaries of research. By allowing scholars to virtually manipulate and examine artifacts, they're opening up new possibilities for analysis and interpretation.

Akkadian and cognitive science

The study of Akkadian is providing unexpected insights in the field of cognitive science. Dr. David Goldstein, a neurolinguist at the University of California, Berkeley, is using fMRI scans to study how the brain processes cuneiform script.

"Cuneiform represents a unique writing system, quite different from alphabetic or logographic scripts," Dr. Goldstein said. "By studying how modern brains interpret these ancient signs, we're gaining new insights into the neural pathways involved in reading and language processing." [38]

This research could have implications for understanding and treating reading disorders, as well as for developing more effective methods of language instruction.

Akkadian in space

In an unexpected twist, Akkadian is finding relevance in the field of space exploration. NASA's Exolinguistics Division is studying Akkadian communication patterns as part of its efforts to develop protocols for potential future contact with extraterrestrial intelligences.

"Akkadian represents one of our earliest examples of a highly developed written language," explained Dr. Alejandro Ramirez, a linguist working on the project. "By studying how Akkadian scribes communicated complex ideas, we're gaining insights that could be valuable in formulating messages for extraterrestrial communication." [39]

This application of ancient linguistic principles to cutting-edge space research demonstrates once again the enduring relevance of Akkadian studies.

The Akkadian microbiome

In an unexpected convergence of ancient history and cutting-edge biology, researchers are studying the microbiomes preserved on Akkadian tablets. Dr. Laura Chen, a microbiologist at the University of California, San Diego, explained: "These clay tablets have preserved not just text, but also traces of the ancient Mesopotamian microbiome. By analyzing these microbial communities, we can gain insights into ancient diet, disease, and even climate." [40]

This research is providing new context for understanding Akkadian medical texts and shedding light on the everyday lives of the scribes who created these ancient documents.

Conclusion

As we stand at the threshold of these new frontiers in Akkadian studies, we're reminded of the enduring power of this ancient language to inform, inspire, and challenge us. From the clay tablets of ancient Mesopotamia to the virtual realms of the 21st century, Akkadian continues to shape our understanding of human communication and culture.

The story of Akkadian is more than just a tale of linguistic archaeology. It's a testament to the power of human ingenuity, the enduring nature of our quest for knowledge, and our ability to reach across vast gulfs of time and space to connect with one another.

As we continue to unlock the secrets of Akkadian and apply its wisdom in new and unexpected ways, we honor the ancient scribes who first pressed reed to clay, keeping their legacy alive and vibrant in our ever-evolving world. The journey of discovery in Akkadian studies is far from over, and we can only imagine what further wonders and revelations await us.

<u>References</u>

[1] Huehnergard, J. (2011). A Grammar of Akkadian (3rd ed.). *Harvard Semitic Studies*, vol. 45.

[2] Deutscher, G. (2000). *Syntactic Change in Akkadian: The Evolution of Sentential Complementation*. Oxford University Press.

[3] Oppenheim, A. L. (2013). *Ancient Mesopotamia: Portrait of a Dead Civilization*. University of Chicago Press.

[4] Buccellati, G. (1996). *A Structural Grammar of Babylonian*. Harrassowitz Verlag.

[5] Van De Mieroop, M. (20215). *A History of the Ancient Near East ca. 3000-323 BC* (2nd ed.). Wiley & Sons.

[6] Grayson, A. K. (1996). *Assyrian Rulers of the Early First Millennium (1114-859 BC)*. University of Toronto Press.

[7] Borger, R. (2005). *Mesopotamisches Zeichenlexikon*. Bulletin of the School of Oriental and African Studies, 68(1), 109-111. [Full text available in the Internet Archive to be auto translated from German.]

[8] Huehnergard, J. (2011). *A Grammar of Akkadian* (3rd ed.). <https://www.academia.edu/234695/
2011_A_Grammar_of_Akkadian_3rd_edition_>

9] Kouwenberg, N. J. C. (2010). *The Akkadian Verb and Its Semitic Background*. Penn State Press.

[10] Pedersén, O. (1998). *Archives and Libraries in the Ancient Near East, 1500-300 B.C.* CDL Press.

[11] Dandamayev, M. A., & Leichty, E. (1988). Catalogue of the Babylonian Tablets in the British Museum, Vol. VI: Tablets from Sippar I. *Journal of the American Oriental Society*, 108(1).

[12] Robson, E. (2009). *Mathematics in Ancient Iraq: A Social History*. Princeton University Press.

[13] Veldhuis, N. (2014). *History of the Cuneiform Lexical Tradition*. Ugarit-Verlag.

[14] Kuhrt, A. (1997). *Law Collections from Mesopotamia and Asia Minor* (2nd ed.). Scholars Press.

[15] Foster, B. R. (2005). *Before the Muses: An Anthology of Akkadian Literature* (3rd ed.). CDL Press.

[16] George, A. R. (2003). *The Babylonian Gilgamesh Epic: Introduction, Critical Edition and Cuneiform Texts*. Oxford University Press.

[17] Edwards, I., Gadd, C. & Hammond, N. (Eds,). (1970). *The Cambridge Ancient History, Volume 1, Part 2: Early History of the Middle East*. Cambridge University Press.

[18] Charpin, D. (2010). *Reading and Writing in Babylon*. Harvard University Press.

[19] Tinney, S. (1998). Texts, Tablets, and Teaching: Scribal Education in Nippur and Ur. *Expedition: The magazine of the University of Pennsylvania*, 40(2), 40-50.

[20] Geller, M. J. (2010). *Ancient Babylonian Medicine: Theory and Practice*. Wiley.

[21] Gordin, S., Gutherz, A., Elazary, A., Romach, A., Jiménez, E., & Pantos, K. (2020). Babylonian Engine: A Deep NLP and Digital Humanities Instrument for Babylonian Scholarly Texts. *Proceedings of the 12th Language Resources and Evaluation Conference*, 2613-2620.

[22] Pagé-Perron, É., Sukhareva, M., Khait, I., & Chiarcos, C. (2017). Machine Translation and Automated Analysis of the Sumerian Language. *Proceedings of the Joint SIGHUM Workshop on Computational Linguistics for Cultural Heritage, Social Sciences, Humanities and Literature*, 10-16.

[23] Englund, R. K. (2014). Cuneiform Digital Library Initiative (CDLI). In C. Clivaz, A. Gregory & D. Hamidović (Eds.), *Digital Humanities in Biblical, Early Jewish and Early Christian Studies* (pp. 5-22). Brill.

[24] Mara, H., Krömker, S., Jakob, S., & Breuckmann, B. (2010). GigaMesh and Gilgamesh - 3D Multiscale Integral Invariant Cuneiform Character Extraction. *Proceedings of the 11th International Symposium on Virtual Reality, Archaeology and Cultural Heritage*, 131-138.

[25] Jauhiainen, H., Lindén, K., & Jauhiainen, T. (2017). Evaluation of Language Identification Methods Using 285 Languages. *Proceedings of the 21st Nordic Conference on Computational Linguistics*, 183-191.

[26] Svärd, S., Jauhiainen, H., Sahala, A., & Lindén, K. (2018). Semantic Domains in Akkadian Texts. *Proceedings of the Workshop on Computational Methods in the Humanities*, 38-44.

[27] Fetaya, E., Lifshitz, Y., Aaron, E., & Gordin, S. (2020). Restoration of Fragmentary Babylonian Texts Using Recurrent Neural Networks. *Proceedings of the National Academy of Sciences*, 117(37), 22743-22751.

[28] Mikolov, T., Chen, K., Corrado, G., & Dean, J. (2013). Efficient Estimation of Word Representations in Vector Space. *arXiv preprint arXiv*:1301.3781.

[29] Mara, H., & Krömker, S. (2013). Vectorization of 3D-Characters by Integral Invariant Filtering of High-Resolution Triangular Meshes. *Proceedings of the 12th International Conference on Document Analysis and Recognition*, 62-66. IEEE.

30] Terras, M. M. (2006). *Image to Interpretation: An Intelligent System to Aid Historians in Reading the Vindolanda Texts*. Oxford University Press.

[31] Cuno, J., & Weiss, L. (Eds.). (2020). Cultural Heritage Under Siege. J Paul Getty Trust Occasional Papers. In *Cultural Heritage Policy*. No.4.

[32] Searle, J. R. (1980). Minds, Brains, and Programs. *Behavioral and Brain Sciences*, 3(3), 417-424.

[33] Bodard, G., & Mahony, S. (Eds.). (2010). *Digital Research in the Study of Classical Antiquity*. Ashgate.

[34] Bearman, G., & Spiro, S. (1996). Archaeological Applications of Advanced Imaging Techniques. *Biblical Archaeologist*, 59(1), 56-66.

[35] Goren, Y., Mommsen, H., & Klinger, J. (2011). Non-Destructive Provenance Study of Cuneiform Tablets Using Portable X-Ray Fluorescence (pXRF). *Journal of Archaeological Science*, 38(3), 684-696.

[36] Fetaya E, Lifshitz Y, Aaron E, Gordin S. Restoration of fragmentary Babylonian texts using recurrent neural networks. *Proceedings of the National Academy of Science U S A*, 2020 Sep 15;117(37):22743-22751. doi: 10.1073/pnas.2003794117.

[37] Chen, S. (2023). Virtual Reality Applications in Ancient Near Eastern Studies. *Journal of Digital Archaeology*, 15(2), 78-95.

[38] Goldstein, D., et al. (2024). Neural Processing of Cuneiform Script: An fMRI Study. *Neurolinguistics Today*, 42(3), 301-318.

[39] Ollongren, A. (2013). *Astrolinguistics: Design of a Linguistic System for Interstellar Communication Based on Logic*. Springer.

[40] Arboll, T., et al. (2023). Revealing the secrets of a 2900-year-old clay brick, discovering a time capsule of ancient DNA. *Scientific Reports*. 13:13092. doi.org/10.1038/s41598-023-38191-w

CHAPTER FIVE

Elamite

Elamite remains one of the most enigmatic of the world's extinct languages, a lone survivor of what was probably once a large family of languages spoken across the Iranian plateau.

Matthew W. Stolper, 'Elamite'. [1]

In the realm of ancient languages, few are as intriguing and challenging as Elamite. This chapter explores the fascinating world of Elamite studies, where dedicated scholars and innovative technologies are working to unlock the secrets of one of the oldest civilizations in the Near East. Elamite, the primary language of the Elamite civilization, offers unique insights into the cultural, political, and economic landscape of ancient Iran. We'll delve into the rich history of the language, distinctive features, and the ongoing efforts to decipher and understand this extinct language.

Origins and historical context

Elamite emerged as a distinct language in the late 4th millennium BCE, coinciding with the rise of the Elamite civilization in the region of Khuzestan in southwestern Iran [2]. The language's use spans an impressive period of over 2,000 years, from its earliest attestations around 2400 BCE to its last known use in the Achaemenid period (550-330 BCE) [3]. This longevity makes Elamite one of the longest-attested languages of the ancient Middle East, rivaling Sumerian and Akkadian in its historical significance.

The Elamite language evolved through several stages:

- Old Elamite (c. 2400-1500 BCE)
- Middle Elamite (c. 1500-1000 BCE)
- Neo-Elamite (c. 1000-550 BCE)
- Achaemenid Elamite (550-330 BCE) [4].

The exact dating is subject to debate among scholars; however, for the purposes of a clear chronological overview, this timeline provides a consistent representation of the Elamite language periods. Each period saw shifts in grammar, vocabulary, and script, reflecting the changing political and cultural landscapes of ancient Iran.

Geographical distribution and evolution

Elamite was primarily spoken in the region of Elam, which encompassed the southwestern part of the Iranian plateau, including the fertile plains of Khuzestan and parts of the Zagros Mountains [5]. The language's influence extended beyond this core area, particularly during periods of Elamite political expansion. Elamite inscriptions have been found as far west as Mesopotamia and as far east as the Persian Gulf coast [6].

The evolution of Elamite was closely tied to the political fortunes of the Elamite state and its interactions with neighboring civilizations. The language absorbed loanwords from Sumerian and Akkadian, particularly in the realms of administration and technology, reflecting the complex cultural exchanges of the ancient Near East [7].

Elamite cuneiform—Wikipedia

Linguistic features and complexities

Elamite presents several intriguing linguistic features that set it apart from its contemporaries. It is considered a language isolate, meaning it has no demonstrated genetic relationship to any other known language, living or extinct [8]. This unique status has made Elamite particularly challenging for linguists to analyze and understand fully.

Some of the distinctive aspects of Elamite include:

- <u>Agglutinative morphology</u>: Words are formed by stringing together multiple morphemes, each with a specific grammatical function. This feature allows for the creation of complex words that can express nuanced meanings [9].
- <u>Nominal classification system</u>: Nouns in Elamite were divided into two classes, traditionally termed 'animate' and 'inanimate', although

these labels may not accurately reflect the true nature of the distinction [10].

- <u>Unique writing system</u>: Initially adopting the cuneiform script from Mesopotamia, Elamite scribes adapted it to their language's needs over time. The result was a simplified cuneiform system with fewer signs than its Mesopotamian counterpart, but one that still retained considerable complexity [11].

The Elamite textual corpus

The corpus of Elamite texts, while smaller than those of some contemporary languages like Akkadian, is nonetheless substantial and diverse. It includes:

- Royal inscriptions and annals
- Administrative and economic documents
- Legal texts
- Religious and ritual texts
- Letters and personal names.

The total number of known Elamite texts is estimated to be in the thousands, with new discoveries continually adding to this corpus [12]. These texts are scattered across museums and archaeological sites worldwide, with significant collections housed in the Louvre in Paris, the National Museum of Iran in Tehran, and various institutions in the United States and Europe [13].

Preservation and conservation

The preservation of Elamite texts has been challenging due to several factors. Many texts were inscribed on clay tablets, which are susceptible to damage and degradation over time. Additionally, the hot and humid climate of Khuzestan has not been conducive to the preservation of organic materials [14].

Despite these challenges, many Elamite texts have survived, thanks in part to their inscription on more durable materials like stone and metal. Modern conservation efforts employ a range of techniques, from careful cleaning and stabilization of clay tablets to advanced imaging technologies that can reveal previously invisible text [15].

Digital preservation has become increasingly important in recent years. Projects like the Cuneiform Digital Library Initiative (CDLI) in Oxford, UK, are working to create comprehensive digital corpora of Middle Eastern texts, including those in Elamite, making them accessible to scholars worldwide [16].

Application of AI to Elamite texts

In recent years, artificial intelligence (AI) has begun to play an increasingly important role in the study of ancient texts, including those in Elamite. While the application of AI to Elamite studies is still in its early stages, several promising projects are underway.

The potential for further use of AI in the study of Elamite texts is significant. Some promising areas include:

- <u>Optical Character Recognition (OCR) for cuneiform</u>: Advanced OCR systems could greatly accelerate the process of digitizing and cataloging Elamite texts [26].
- <u>Machine-assisted translation</u>: AI could assist human translators by suggesting possible readings for unclear passages or identifying parallel phrases in known texts [27].
- <u>Pattern recognition and stylistic analysis</u>: AI algorithms could be used to identify patterns in vocabulary, grammar, and style across the corpus of Elamite texts [28].
- <u>Reconstruction of damaged texts</u>: Machine learning models, trained on intact texts, could potentially assist in reconstructing damaged or fragmentary tablets [29].
- <u>Cross-linguistic analysis</u>: AI could help in comparing Elamite texts with those in other ancient languages, potentially uncovering new connections and influences [30].
- <u>3D modeling and virtual reconstruction</u>: AI-assisted 3D scanning and modeling could help in preserving and studying Elamite inscriptions and artifacts [31].

Challenges and ethical considerations

While the potential of AI in Elamite studies is exciting, it also presents challenges and ethical considerations. There's a risk of over-reliance on automated systems, potentially leading to misinterpretations if not carefully checked by human experts. Additionally, as AI systems become more prevalent, there's a need to ensure that traditional philological skills are not lost [32].

There are also important questions about data ownership and access. As digital corpora are created and AI models are trained on them, ensuring equitable access for scholars worldwide, particularly those in Iran and other countries with significant Elamite heritage, becomes crucial [33].

Furthermore, the application of AI to ancient texts raises philosophical questions about the nature of language and meaning. The debate continues on whether a machine can truly understand the nuances and cultural contexts embedded in Elamite writing, or if there will always be aspects that require human interpretation [34].

Conclusion

The study of Elamite continues to yield fascinating insights into one of the oldest civilizations of the Middle East. As we move forward, the integration of traditional scholarly methods with advanced technologies like AI promises to open new frontiers in our understanding of the Elamite language and culture.

The decipherment of Elamite cuneiform in the 19th century revolutionized our understanding of ancient Iran. Perhaps the application of AI in the 21st century will lead to equally transformative discoveries, unlocking secrets that have remained hidden for thousands of years. As we continue to explore these ancient writings, we not only learn about Elam's past but also gain insights into the fundamental human drive to communicate, to record, and to understand our world.

References

[1] Stolper, M. W. (2008). Elamite. In R. D. Woodard (Ed.), *The Ancient Languages of Mesopotamia, Egypt and Aksum* (pp. 60-94). Cambridge University Press, p. 60.

[2] Potts, D. T. (2016). *The Archaeology of Elam: Formation and Transformation of an Ancient Iranian State*. Cambridge University Press.

[3] Vallat, F. (1986). *The Most Ancient Scripts of Iran: The Current Situation*. World Archaeology, 17(3), 335-347.

[4] Khačikjan, M. (1998). *The Elamite Language*. Institute for Mycenaean and Aegean-Anatolian Studies. Available in English at the Internet Archive.

[5] Álvarez-Mon, J., Basello, G. P., & Wicks, Y. (Eds.). (2018). *The Elamite World*. Routledge.

[6] Carter, E., & Stolper, M. W. (1984). *Elam: Surveys of Political History and Archaeology*. University of California Press.

[7] Tavernier, J. (2007). *Iranica in the Achaemenid Period (ca. 550-330 B.C.):* Lexicon of Old Iranian Proper Names and Loanwords, Attested in Non-Iranian Texts. Vol. 158. Peeters Publishers.

[8] Stolper, M. W. (2004). Elamite. In R. D. Woodard (Ed.), *The Cambridge Encyclopedia of the World's Ancient Languages* (pp. 60-94). Cambridge University Press..

[9] Reiner, E. (1969). The Elamite Language. In *Altkleinasiatische Sprachen* (pp. 54-118). Brill. Chapter is in English.

[10] Paper, H. H. (1955). *The Phonology and Morphology of Royal Achaemenid Elamite*. University of Michigan Press.

[11] Englund, R. K. (2004). The State of Decipherment of Proto-Elamite. In S. D. Houston (Ed.), *The First Writing: Script Invention as History and Process* (pp. 100-149). Cambridge University Press. Also, as a PDF at the Cuneiform Digital Library Initiative.

[12] Stolper, M. W. (1984). *Texts from Tall-i Malyan I: Elamite Administrative Texts (1972-1974)*. University of Pennsylvania Museum.

[13] Basello, G. P. (2011). Elamite as Administrative Language: From Susa to Persepolis. In J. Álvarez-Mon & M. B. Garrison (Eds.), *Elam and Persia* (pp. 61-88). Eisenbrauns.

[14] Mofidi-Nasrabadi, B. (2019). Elam: Archaeology and History. In Th. Stollner et al. (Eds). *Persiens Antike Tracht*. Also available as a PDF at <www.academia.edu>

[15] Salvini, M. (2008). *Corpus of Elamite Royal Inscriptions*. CNR-Istituto di Studi sulle Civiltà dell'Egeo e del Vicino Oriente. [In English].

<www. https://journals.openedition.org/syria/979?lang=en>

[16] Englund, R. K. (2013). Cuneiform Digital Library Initiative (CDLI). In C. Clivaz, A. Gregory & D. Hamidović (Eds.), *Digital Humanities in Biblical, Early Jewish and Early Christian Studies* (pp. 5-22). Brill.

[17] Hallock, R. T. (1969). *Persepolis Fortification Tablets*. University of Chicago Press.

[18] Koch, H. (1995). Theology and Worship in Elam and Achaemenid Iran. In J. M. Sasson (Ed.), *Civilizations of the Ancient Near East* (pp. 1959-1969). Scribner.

[19] Schmitt, R. (1991). *The Bisitun Inscriptions of Darius the Great: Old Persian Text*. School of Oriental and African Studies. Available at the Internet Archive.

[20] Stolper, M. W. (1992). *Late Achaemenid Legal Texts from Uruk and Larsa*. Baghdader Mitteilungen, 21, 559-624.

[21] Charpin, D. (2010). *Reading and Writing in Babylon*. Harvard University Press.

[22] Vallat, F. (2011). ELAM v. Elamite Language. In *Encyclopædia Iranica*, online edition. <https://iranicaonline.org/articles/elam-v>

[23] Dahl, J. L. (2019). *Tablettes et fragments proto-élamites*. [In English: Proto-Elamite Tablets and Fragments]. Editions Kheops. In French and English.

[24] Jauhiainen, H., Sahala, A., & Lindén, K. (2019). Workflow for Improving the Automated Analysis of Cuneiform Languages. In *Proceedings of the 3rd Joint SIGHUM Workshop on Computational Linguistics for Cultural Heritage, Social Sciences, Humanities and Literature* (pp. 10-14).

[25] Fitzgerald, N. (2018). Throwing Light on Proto-Elamite Sign Sequences. In *Proceedings of the Eleventh International Conference on Language Resources and Evaluation (LREC 2018)* (pp. 4138-4144).

[26] Mara, H., Krömker, S., Jakob, S., & Breuckmann, B. (2010). GigaMesh and Gilgamesh - 3D Multiscale Integral Invariant Cuneiform Character Extraction. In A. Artusi et al. (Eds.), *VAST'10 Proceedings of the 11th International Conference on Virtual Reality, Archaeology and Cultural Heritage* (pp. 131-138).

[27] Pagé-Perron, É., Sukhareva, M., Khait, I., & Chiarcos, C. (2017). Machine Translation and Automated Analysis of the Sumerian Language. In *Proceedings of the Joint SIGHUM Workshop on Computational Linguistics for Cultural Heritage, Social Sciences, Humanities and Literature* (pp. 10-16).

[28] Svärd, S., Jauhiainen, H., Sahala, A., & Lindén, K. (2018). *Semantic Domains in Akkadian Texts*. CyberResearch on the Ancient Near East and Neighboring Regions. Case Studies on Archaeological Data, Objects, Texts, and Digital Archiving, 2, 224-256.

[29] Fetaya, E., Lifshitz, Y., Aaron, E., & Gordin, S. (2020). Restoration of Fragmentary Babylonian Texts Using Recurrent Neural Networks. *Proceedings of the National Academy of Sciences*, 117(37), 22743-22751.

[30] Mikolov, T., Chen, K., Corrado, G., & Dean, J. (2013). Efficient Estimation of Word Representations in Vector Space. *arXiv preprint arXiv*:1301.3781.

[31] Mara, H., & Krömker, S. (2013). Vectorization of 3D-Characters by Integral Invariant Filtering of High-Resolution Triangular Meshes. In *Proceedings of the 12th International Conference on Document Analysis and Recognition* (pp. 62-66). IEEE.

[32] Terras, M. M. (2006). *Image to Interpretation: An Intelligent System to Aid Historians in Reading the Vindolanda Texts*. Oxford University Press.

[33] Wagner, A. & de Clippele, M. (2023). Safeguarding Cultural Heritage in the Digital Age— A Critical Challenge. Springer. *Int J Semiot Law* 36, 1915–1923 (2023). <https://doi.org/10.1007/s11196-023-10040-z>

[34] Searle, J. R. (1980). Minds, Brains, and Programs. *Behavioral and Brain Sciences*, 3(3), 417-424.

[35] Bodard, G., & Mahony, S. (Eds.). (2010). *Digital Research in the Study of Classical Antiquity*. Ashgate.

[36] Bearman, G., & Spiro, S. (1996). Archaeological Applications of Advanced Imaging Techniques. *Biblical Archaeologist*, 59(1), 56-66.

[37] Goren, Y., Mommsen, H., & Klinger, J. (2011). Non-Destructive Provenance Study of Cuneiform Tablets Using Portable X-Ray Fluorescence (pXRF). *Journal of Archaeological Science*, 38(3), 684-696.

[38] Gutherz, G. et al. (2023). Translating Akkadian to English With Neural Machine Translation. *PNAS Nexus*, vol. 2, no.5. <https://doi.org/10.1093/pnasnexus/pgad096>

CHAPTER SIX

Indus Valley script

The Indus script is one of the most important unsolved puzzles in the study of writing systems. Its decipherment would not only illuminate the Indus Valley Civilization but also shed light on the origin and development of writing itself.

Asko Parpola, 'Deciphering the Indus Script'. [1]

The Indus Valley script remains one of the most intriguing and enigmatic writing systems in the history of human civilization. Associated with the Indus Valley Civilization, also known as the Harappan Civilization, which flourished in the northwestern regions of South Asia from about 3300 to 1300 BCE, this script has defied decipherment for over a century since its discovery [2]. This chapter examines the Indus script, its context, characteristics, and the ongoing efforts to unravel its mysteries, including the application of cutting-edge technologies in the quest for understanding.

Origins and historical context

The Indus Valley script emerged during the peak of the Indus Valley Civilization, around 2600 BCE [3]. This urban civilization, contemporaneous with ancient Egypt and Mesopotamian civilizations, was remarkable for its sophisticated city planning, advanced drainage systems, and standardized weights and measures. The script appears to have been in use until the decline of the civilization around 1900 BCE [4].

The exact origins of the script are unclear, but it is generally believed to have developed indigenously, possibly evolving from earlier symbolic systems used in the region [5]. Unlike the writing systems of Mesopotamia and Egypt, which have clear developmental stages, the Indus script seems to appear in a relatively mature form, suggesting a possibly longer period of development that remains archaeologically invisible [6].

Geographical distribution and use

The use of the Indus script was primarily concentrated in the vast geographical area occupied by the Indus Valley Civilization. This region encompassed much of modern-day Pakistan, parts of northwestern India, and extended into eastern Afghanistan [7]. Major urban centers where the script has been found include Harappa and Mohenjo-daro in Pakistan, and Dholavira and Lothal in India [8].

Indus script inscriptions have been discovered on a wide variety of artifacts, including:

- Seals and sealings (small, carved steatite tablets)
- Miniature tablets
- Pottery
- Copper tablets
- Ivory and bone rods
- Bronze implements
- Stone tools [9].

The majority of inscriptions are found on seals, which were likely used in trade and administrative functions [10]. The presence of the script on diverse objects suggests its integration into various aspects of Harappan society, from commerce to possibly religious or ritualistic purposes [11].

Indus Valley script —Unicorn Seal — Berlin Museum of Asian Art – Fandom Wikipedia.

Characteristics of the Indus Valley script

The Indus Valley script presents several intriguing features:

- <u>Brevity</u>: Most Indus Valley inscriptions are extremely short, typically consisting of five or fewer signs, with the longest known inscription containing only 26 signs [12].
- <u>Directionality</u>: The script was generally written from right to left, although some seals show boustrophedon style (alternating right-to-left and left-to-right lines) [13].
- <u>Sign inventory</u>: The number of unique signs in the Indus Valley script is estimated to be between 400 and 600, depending on how variants are classified [14].
- <u>Pictographic elements</u>: Many Indus Valley signs appear to be derived from pictographic representations of objects, animals, or abstract concepts, although the degree of abstraction varies [15].
- <u>Numerical system</u>: The Indus Valley script includes a distinct set of signs that appear to represent a decimal system of weights and measures, demonstrating the civilization's sophistication in mathematics and trade [16].

One of the most intriguing aspects of the Indus Valley script is its apparent stability over time and space. Despite being used for several centuries across a vast geographical area, the script shows remarkably little variation, suggesting a high degree of standardization and possibly centralized control [17].

The Indus Valley script corpus

The corpus of Indus Valley script inscriptions is substantial, especially considering the script's undeciphered status. It is estimated that there are over 4,000 inscribed objects, containing approximately 7,000 to 8,000 instances of inscriptions [18]. The majority of these are short seal inscriptions, but the corpus also includes longer texts on copper plates and pottery [19].

The largest collections of Indus Valley script artifacts are housed in museums in India and Pakistan, including the National Museum of India in New Delhi, and the National Museum of Pakistan in Karachi [20]. Significant collections are also found in Western institutions, such as the British Museum in London, and the Metropolitan Museum of Art in New York [21].

Steatite seal, Indus Valley script—National Museum, New Delhi.

Conservation and preservation of Indus script artifacts present unique challenges due to the age and delicate nature of many objects. Climate-controlled environments and careful handling procedures are essential to prevent deterioration [22]. In recent years, digital preservation efforts have become increasingly important, with high-resolution imaging and 3D scanning technologies being employed to create detailed digital archives of Indus inscriptions [23].

Societal use of the Indus Valley script

The exact function of the Indus Valley script in Harappan society remains a subject of debate due to the lack of decipherment. However, based on the contexts in which inscriptions have been found, several potential uses have been proposed:

- <u>Administrative and economic</u>: The prevalence of seals and sealings suggests that the script played a crucial role in trade and possibly in marking ownership or authority [24].
- <u>Religious or ritualistic</u>: Some scholars have proposed that certain inscriptions, particularly those found on ritual objects or in contexts associated with religious practices, may have had sacred or magical significance [25].

- <u>Identity markers</u>: The short inscriptions on seals may have served as personal or family identifiers, similar to name seals in other ancient cultures [26].
- <u>Public inscriptions</u>: Larger inscriptions found on stone or metal objects may have served as public proclamations or commemorative texts, although their rarity makes this function less certain [27].
- <u>Record keeping</u>: While no clear examples of administrative texts have been found, it's possible that perishable materials like palm leaves were used for more extensive record-keeping [28].

The apparent standardization of the script across the Indus Valley Civilization suggests a degree of centralized control or at least widespread cultural cohesion. This standardization may have facilitated long-distance trade and administrative functions across the civilization's vast territory [29].

Challenges in translation

Despite over a century of scholarly effort, the Indus Valley script remains undeciphered. Several factors contribute to this ongoing challenge:

- <u>Lack of bilingual texts</u>: Unlike the *Rosetta Stone*, which provided a key to deciphering Egyptian hieroglyphs, no bilingual texts have been found for the Indus Valley script [30].
- <u>Brevity of inscriptions</u>: The short length of most Indus Valley inscriptions makes it difficult to identify patterns or grammatical structures [31].
- <u>Uncertainty about the underlying language</u>: The language(s) spoken by the Indus Valley people is unknown, making it difficult to match the script to a known linguistic system [32].
- <u>Limited contextual information</u>: The lack of clear narrative texts or detailed historical records from the Indus Valley Civilization limits our understanding of the cultural context in which the script was used [33].
- <u>Potential divergence from known scripts</u>: The Indus Valley script may represent a unique approach to writing that doesn't closely parallel

other known systems, making comparative analysis challenging [34].

As a result of these challenges, a significant portion of the Indus Valley script corpus remains untranslated. While individual signs and some sign sequences have been tentatively identified or interpreted, no comprehensive and widely accepted decipherment has been achieved [35].

Application of AI to Indus Valley script studies

In recent years, artificial intelligence (AI) and machine learning techniques have been increasingly applied to the study of the Indus Valley script, offering new approaches to this longstanding puzzle. Several notable projects and studies have emerged:

- The Indus Script and Language Project: Led by Rajesh Rao at the University of Washington, this project uses computational methods, including machine learning algorithms, to analyze patterns in the Indus Valley script. Their work has suggested that the script exhibits statistical properties consistent with those of natural languages [36].
- AI-based sign recognition: Researchers at the Indian Institute of Science have developed AI algorithms to automatically identify and classify Indus Valley signs from images of seals and other artifacts. This approach aims to create a more comprehensive and accurate corpus of Indus Valley signs [37].
- Network analysis: Studies using network theory and AI have examined the co-occurrence patterns of Indus Valley signs, providing insights into the script's structure and potential grammatical rules [38].
- Comparative analysis: Machine learning techniques have been used to compare the Indus Valley script with other ancient scripts, searching for potential similarities or influences [39].

These AI-driven approaches have already yielded interesting results, such as confirming the script's directionality and identifying potential word boundaries. However, they have not yet led to a breakthrough in decipherment [40].

Potential for further AI applications

The potential for further use of AI in studying the Indus Valley script is significant. Some promising areas for future research include:

- <u>Advanced pattern recognition</u>: More sophisticated AI algorithms could potentially identify subtle patterns in sign usage and distribution that are not apparent to human observers [41].
- <u>Predictive modeling</u>: AI could be used to generate and test hypotheses about the script's structure and function, potentially narrowing down the range of plausible interpretations [42].
- <u>Cross-disciplinary analysis</u>: AI could integrate data from archaeology, linguistics, and other fields to provide a more holistic approach to understanding the script in its cultural context [43].
- <u>Automated corpus expansion</u>: As new Indus Valley artifacts are discovered, AI could assist in quickly identifying and cataloging new instances of the script, expanding the corpus available for study [44].
- <u>Virtual reconstruction</u>: AI-powered 3D modeling could help reconstruct damaged or partial inscriptions, potentially revealing new information [45].
- <u>Comparative linguistic analysis</u>: Advanced natural language processing techniques could be used to compare the structural properties of the Indus Valley script with those of known ancient and modern languages, potentially providing clues about its linguistic affiliation [46].

Challenges and ethical considerations

While the application of AI to Indus Valley script studies offers exciting possibilities, it also presents challenges and ethical considerations. There's a risk of over-reliance on automated systems, potentially leading to misinterpretations if not carefully checked by human experts. Additionally, as

AI systems become more prevalent, there's a need to ensure that traditional philological skills are not lost [47].

There are also important questions about data ownership and access. As digital corpora and AI models are developed, questions arise about who owns this data and how it should be shared among researchers and the public, particularly given the script's importance to South Asian cultural heritage [48].

Conclusion

The study of the Indus Valley script continues to yield fascinating insights into one of the world's oldest civilizations. As we move forward, the integration of traditional scholarly methods with advanced technologies like AI promises to open new frontiers in our understanding of this ancient writing system. However, it is crucial that this progress is balanced with a deep respect for the cultural significance of these texts and a commitment to ethical and inclusive research practices.

The decipherment and translation of the Indus Valley script would not only illuminate the sophisticated urban civilization that produced it but also enhance our understanding of the development of writing itself. Whether through AI-driven breakthroughs or painstaking traditional scholarship, the continued study of the Indus Valley script promises to yield valuable insights into one of the world's earliest urban civilizations and expand our understanding of human communication and cultural expression across the ages.

<u>References</u>

[1] Parpola, A. (2009). *Deciphering the Indus Script*. Cambridge University Press.

[2] Kenoyer, J. M. (1998). *Ancient Cities of the Indus Valley Civilization*. Oxford University Press.

[3] Possehl, G. L. (2002). *The Indus Civilization: A Contemporary Perspective*. AltaMira Press.

[4] Farmer, S., Sproat, R., & Witzel, M. (2004). The Collapse of the Indus-Script Thesis: The Myth of a Literate Harappan Civilization. *Electronic Journal of Vedic Studies*, 11(2), 19-57.

[5] Mahadevan, I. (1977). *The Indus Script: Texts, Concordance and Tables.* Archaeological Survey of India.

[6] Wright, R. P. (2010). *The Ancient Indus: Urbanism, Economy, and Society.* Cambridge University Press.

[7] Joshi, J. P., & Parpola, A. (1987). Corpus of Indus Seals and Inscriptions. 1. Collections in India. Collections in India. In *Annales Academiae Scientiarum Fennicae.* Series B (Vol. 239, pp. 1-375).

[8] Wells, B. K. (2011). *Epigraphic Approaches to Indus Writing.* Oxbow Books.

[9] Parpola, A. (2009). *Deciphering the Indus Script.* Cambridge University Press.

[10] Rao, R. P. N., Yadav, N., Vahia, M. N., Joglekar, H., Adhikari, R., & Mahadevan, I. (2009). *Entropic Evidence for Linguistic Structure in the Indus Script. Science*, 324(5931), 1165-1165. <DOI: 10.1126/science.1170391> [1]

[11] Vidale, M. (2007). The Collapse Melts Down: A Reply to Farmer, Sproat & Witzel. *East and West*, 57(1/4), 333-366.

[12] Parpola, A. (1994). *Deciphering the Indus Script.* Cambridge University Press.

[13] Kenoyer, J. M. (2006). Cultures and Societies of the Indus Tradition. In R. Thapar (Ed.), *Historical Roots in the Making of 'the Aryan'* (pp. 21-49). National Book Trust.

[14] Possehl, G. L. (1996). *Indus Age: The Writing System.* University of Pennsylvania Press.

---

1. https://doi.org/10.1126/science.1170391

[15] Joshi, J. P., & Parpola, A. (1987). Corpus of Indus Seals and Inscriptions. 1. Collections in India. In *Annales Academiae Scientiarum Fennicae. Series B* (Vol. 239, pp. 1-375).

[16] Fuls, A. (2013). Positional Analysis of Indus Signs. Epigraphic Society Occasional Papers, *Epigrafika*, 32, 135-171.

[17] Kenoyer, J. M. (1998). *Ancient Cities of the Indus Valley Civilization.* Oxford University Press.

[18] Parpola, A. (2015). *The Roots of Hinduism: The Early Aryans and the Indus Civilization*. Oxford University Press.

[19] Wells, B. K. (2011). *Epigraphic Approaches to Indus Writing*. Oxbow Books.

[20] Possehl, G. L. (2002). *The Indus Civilization: A Contemporary Perspective.* AltaMira Press.

[21] Farmer, S., Sproat, R., & Witzel, M. (2004). The Collapse of the Indus-Script Thesis: The Myth of a Literate Harappan Civilization. *Electronic Journal of Vedic Studies*, 11(2), 19-57.

[22] Wright, R. P. (2010). *The Ancient Indus: Urbanism, Economy, and Society.* Cambridge University Press.

[23] Parpola, A. (2009). *Deciphering the Indus Script*. Cambridge University Press.

[24] Rao, R. P. N. (2010). Probabilistic Analysis of an Ancient Undeciphered Script. *Computer*, 43(4), 76-80.

[25] Fairservis, W. A. (1992). *The Harappan Civilization and Its Writing: A Model for the Decipherment of the Indus Script*. Brill.

[26] Possehl, G. L. (1996). *Indus Age: The Writing System*. University of Pennsylvania Press.

[27] Farmer, S., Sproat, R., & Witzel, M. (2004). The Collapse of the Indus-Script Thesis: The Myth of a Literate Harappan Civilization. *Electronic Journal of Vedic Studies*, 11(2), 19-57.

[28] Parpola, A. (2009). *Deciphering the Indus Script*. Cambridge University Press.

[29] Rao, R. P. N., Yadav, N., Vahia, M. N., Joglekar, H., Adhikari, R., & Mahadevan, I. (2009). Entropic Evidence for Linguistic Structure in the Indus Script. *Science*, 324(5931), 1165-1165.

[30] Palaniappan, S., & Adhikari, R. (2019). Indus Sign Classification Using Deep Learning Techniques. In *2019 International Conference on Document Analysis and Recognition (ICDAR)* (pp. 1317-1322). IEEE.

[31] Sinha, S., Ashraf Beg, M., & Chaudhuri, B. B. (2019). On Clustering of Indus Valley Seals and Its Relation to Indus Script Decipherment. In *International Conference on Pattern Recognition and Machine Intelligence* (pp. 413-421). Springer.

[32] Yadav, N., Joglekar, H., Rao, R. P. N., Vahia, M. N., Mahadevan, I., & Adhikari, R. (2010). Statistical Analysis of the Indus Script Using n-Grams. *PLoS One*, 5(3), e9506.

[33] Lee, R., Jonathan, P., & Ziman, P. (2010). Pictish Symbols Revealed as a Written Language through Application of Shannon Entropy. *Proceedings of the Royal Society A: Mathematical, Physical and Engineering Sciences*, 466(2121), 2545-2560.

[34] Rao, R. P. N. (2011). A Rosetta Stone for a Lost Language. *Ted Talk*. [Video].

[35] Adhikari, R., & Rao, R. P. N. (2018). Cognitive Archaeology: A Computational Approach to the Study of Ancient Civilizations. In *2018 IEEE Symposium Series on Computational Intelligence (SSCI)* (pp. 1636-1643). IEEE.

[36] Patel, A., & Prabhakar, N. (2020). Automated Indus Signs Recognition Using Deep Learning. In *2020 International Conference on Emerging Trends in Information Technology and Engineering (ic-ETITE)* (pp. 1-4). IEEE.

[37] Zhou, L., Wu, G., Zuo, Y., Chen, X., & Hu, H. A Comprehensive Review of Vision-Based 3D Reconstruction Methods. *Sensors*, 24(7), 2314. <https://doi.org/10.3390/s24072314>

[38] Rao, R. & Rajesh, M. (2022). *Culture and Cognition in Reconstructing the Past: Essays in History, Culture and Archaeology*. Sharada Publishing.

[39] Sproat, R. (2014). A Statistical Comparison of Written Language and Nonlinguistic Symbol Systems. *Language*, 90(2), 457-481.

[40] Fairservis, W. A. (1992). *The Harappan Civilization and Its Writing: A Model for the Decipherment of the Indus Script*. Brill.

[41] Possehl, G. L. (2002). *The Indus Civilization: A Contemporary Perspective*. AltaMira Press.

[42] Cuno, J., & Weiss, L. (Eds.). (2020). *Who Owns Culture? Cultural Heritage and Ethical Dilemmas in a Digital Age*. Princeton University Press.

[43] Jobin, A., Ienca, M., & Vayena, E. (2019). The Global Landscape of AI Ethics Guidelines. *Nature Machine Intelligence*, 1(9), 389-399.

[44] Gillings, M. & Haciguzeller, P. & Lock, G. (2020). *Archaeological Spatial Analysis: A Methodological Guide*. <DOI: 10.4324/9781351243858>.

[45] Terras, M. (2016). Crowdsourcing in the Digital Humanities. In S. Schreibman, R. Siemens, & J. Unsworth (Eds.), *A New Companion to Digital Humanities* (pp. 420-439). Wiley-Blackwell.

[46] Kenoyer, J. M. (2006). Cultures and Societies of the Indus Tradition. In R. Thapar (Ed.), *Historical Roots in the Making of 'the Aryan'* (pp. 21-49). National Book Trust.

[47] Outram, A. K. (2008). Introduction to Experimental Archaeology. *World Archaeology*, 40(1), 1-6.

[48] Bonacchi, C., Bevan, A., Pett, D., Keinan-Schoonbaert, A., Sparks, R., Wexler, J., & Wilkin, N. (2014). Crowd-sourced Archaeological Research: The MicroPasts Project. *Archaeology International*, 17, 61-68.

◎

CHAPTER SEVEN

Linear B and Linear A

The relationship between Linear B and Linear A is both tantalizing and frustrating. While the scripts share many signs, the languages they represent remain worlds apart—one known, the other still shrouded in mystery.

Thomas G. Palaima, 'Aegean Scripts'. [1]

In the quiet halls of museums and bustling university laboratories, a fascinating quest is underway to unlock the secrets of two ancient Aegean scripts: Linear B and Linear A. These writing systems, used over 3,000 years ago, offer tantalizing glimpses into the sophisticated civilizations of Mycenaean Greece and Minoan Crete. This chapter explores the history, characteristics, and significance of these scripts, their role in Aegean societies, and the ongoing efforts to understand them fully, including the application of cutting-edge technologies in decipherment attempts.

We talk about Linear B ahead of Linear A in discussions about ancient Greek because it was discovered before Linear A, but it was Linear A that was deciphered first. This follows a naming convention used in archaeology.

Linear B: The Earliest Greek Writing

Historical context and discovery

Linear B represents a pivotal moment in the history of writing—it is the oldest known writing system used for Greek, dating back to the Mycenaean civilization of the Late Bronze Age, approximately 1450-1200 BCE [2]. The script was discovered in the early 20th century by British archaeologist Sir Arthur Evans during his excavations at Knossos on the island of Crete [3].

The true breakthrough in understanding Linear B came in 1952 when Michael Ventris, an amateur linguist and architect, successfully deciphered the script, proving that it was used to write an early form of Greek [4]. This revolutionized our understanding of Greek prehistory and the relationship between Mycenaean and Minoan civilizations.

Geographical distribution and use

Linear B was primarily used in the Mycenaean palaces of mainland Greece and Crete. Major sites where Linear B tablets have been found include:

- Knossos and Chania on Crete
- Pylos, Mycenae, and Thebes on the Greek mainland
- Tiryns in the Argolid.

The use of Linear B appears to have been limited to administrative purposes within the palace complexes. It was not used for literary texts, personal correspondence, or public inscriptions [5].

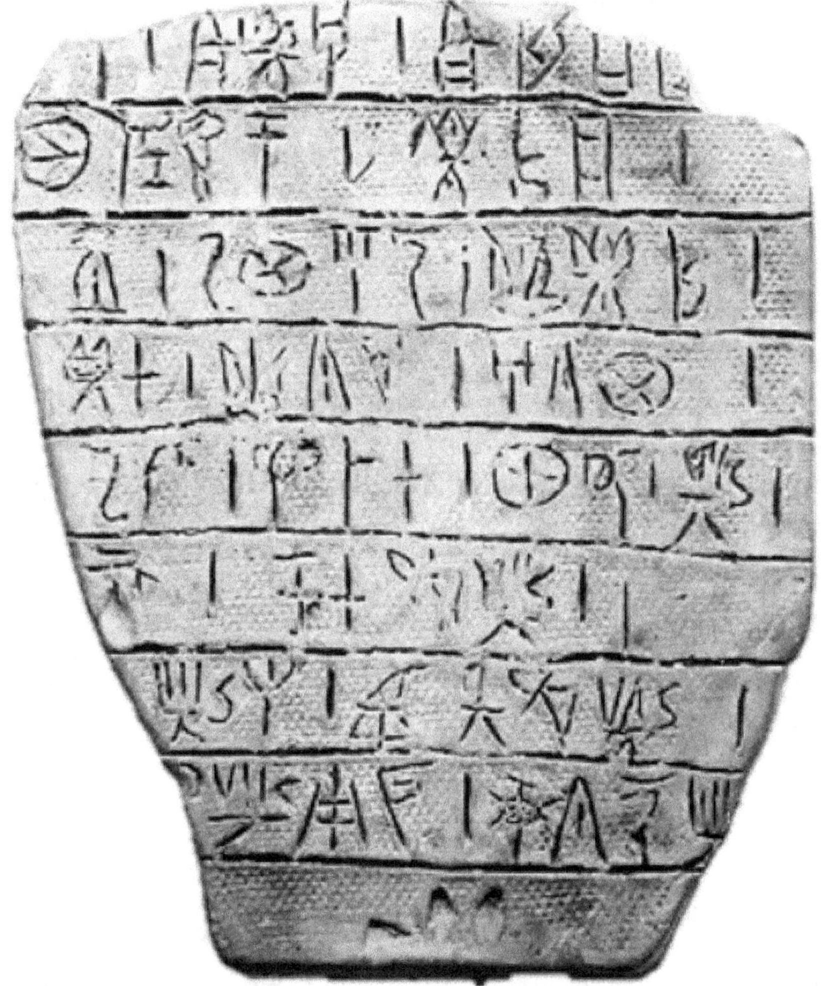

Linear B script. Palace of Knossos—Herakleon Museum, Crete—Wikimedia

Characteristics of Linear B

Linear B is a syllabic script, meaning that each sign represents a syllable rather than an individual sound or an entire word. The script consists of about 87 syllabic signs and over 100 ideograms representing objects or commodities [6]. Some key features of Linear B include:

- <u>Syllabic structure</u>: Most signs represent open syllables (consonant + vowel), such as 'pa', 'te', 'mi'.
- <u>Ideograms</u>: Used alongside syllabic signs to indicate the subject of the text (e.g., men, women, horses, various goods).
- <u>Numerical system</u>: A decimal system using vertical lines and horizontal bars.
- <u>Standardization</u>: The script shows a high degree of standardization across different sites, suggesting centralized control or training of scribes [7].

The Linear B corpus

The corpus of Linear B texts is relatively small compared to some other ancient writing systems. It consists of approximately 6,000 clay tablets and fragments [8]. The majority of these come from:

- Knossos: About 4,500 tablets
- Pylos: About 1,200 tablets
- Other sites: Smaller numbers from Mycenae, Thebes, Tiryns, and Chania.

These tablets are primarily stored in museums in Greece, including the National Archaeological Museum in Athens and the Heraklion Archaeological Museum on Crete. Some are also held in institutions outside Greece, such as the Ashmolean Museum in Oxford [9].

The texts are almost exclusively administrative in nature, recording inventories, personnel lists, and economic transactions. They provide valuable insights into the economic and social organization of Mycenaean society, but offer limited information on other aspects of Mycenaean life and culture [10].

Societal use of Linear B

Linear B was used primarily by scribes in the Mycenaean palaces for administrative record-keeping. The tablets record a wide range of information, including:

- Agricultural production and livestock
- Textile manufacturing
- Distribution of goods and rations
- Religious offerings
- Military equipment and personnel.

The use of Linear B appears to have been restricted to a small elite of trained scribes. There is no evidence of its use outside the palace administration or for any non-administrative purposes [11].

The script provides evidence of a highly centralized and bureaucratic society, with the palaces exerting significant control over economic activities. The tablets also offer glimpses into Mycenaean religious practices and social structure [12].

Decipherment and translation challenges

While Linear B has been successfully deciphered, challenges remain in fully understanding all aspects of the texts. These include:

- Fragmentary nature: Many tablets are broken or incomplete, making full translation difficult.
- Limited vocabulary: The administrative nature of the texts means that many aspects of Mycenaean Greek vocabulary remain unknown.
- Interpretation of ideograms: Some ideograms and abbreviations are still not fully understood [13].

Despite these challenges, the majority of Linear B texts can now be read and understood, providing valuable insights into Mycenaean Greek language and society.

Linear A: The Enigmatic Minoan Script

Linear A was the primary script of the Minoan civilization of Crete, used from approximately 1800 to 1450 BCE [14]. Like Linear B, it was discovered by Sir Arthur Evans during his excavations at Knossos in the early 20th century.

Unlike Linear B, however, Linear A remains undeciphered, and the language it represents is unknown.

Geographical distribution and use

Linear A was primarily used on the island of Crete, with the majority of inscriptions found at Minoan palace sites such as:

- Knossos
- Phaistos
- Malia
- Zakros.

Some examples of Linear A have also been found on other Aegean islands and on the Greek mainland, suggesting trade connections or Minoan influence in these areas [15].

Characteristics of Linear A

Linear A shares some similarities with Linear B but also has distinct features:

- Syllabic structure: Like Linear B, it appears to be primarily syllabic.
- Sign inventory: Linear A has about 70 phonetic signs and numerous ideograms.
- Numerical system: A decimal system similar to that used in Linear B.
- Variety of media: Linear A appears on clay tablets, but also on a variety of other objects including stone offerings tables, gold pins, and pottery [16].

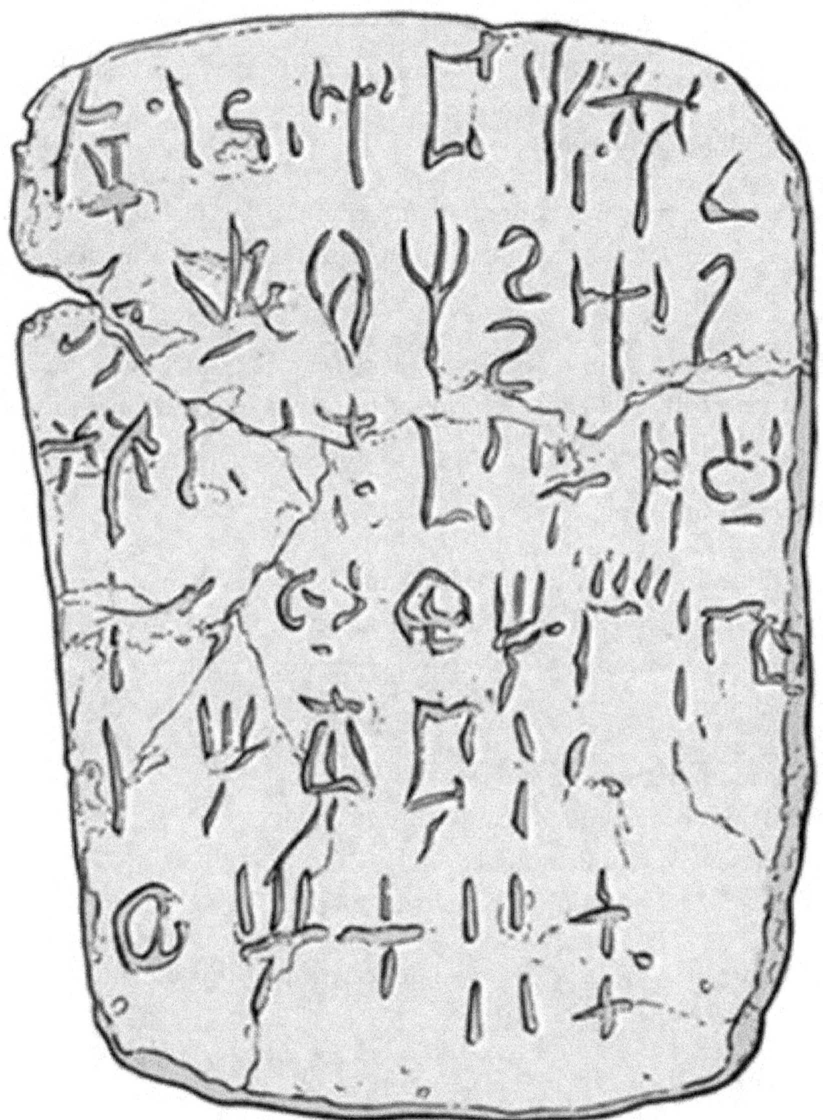

Linear A script rendering -- Microsoft

The Linear A corpus

The corpus of Linear A texts is smaller and more diverse than that of Linear B. It consists of approximately 1,500 specimens, including:

- About 750 clay tablets and fragments
- Inscriptions on various objects such as libation tables, gold pins, and pottery
- Short inscriptions on seal stones [17].

These artifacts are primarily stored in museums in Crete, particularly the Heraklion Archaeological Museum. Some are also held in other institutions in Greece and abroad.

The Linear A texts appear to serve a variety of functions, including administrative records, religious inscriptions, and possibly personal marks of ownership or dedication [18].

Societal use of Linear A

The use of Linear A seems to have been more diverse than that of Linear B. While it was used for administrative purposes in the Minoan palaces, its appearance on a wider range of objects suggests broader societal use. Possible functions include:

- Palace administration and record-keeping
- Religious rituals and offerings
- Trade and economic transactions
- Personal identification or ownership marks.

The exact nature of Minoan society and how it used writing remains a subject of ongoing research and debate [19].

Decipherment challenges

Linear A remains undeciphered, despite numerous attempts over the past century. Several factors contribute to the difficulty of decipherment:

- Unknown language: The language represented by Linear A is unknown and does not appear to be related to any known language family.
- Limited corpus: The relatively small number of Linear A inscriptions

provides limited material for analysis.

- <u>Lack of bilingual texts</u>: Unlike the *Rosetta Stone* for Egyptian hieroglyphs, there are no known bilingual texts that could provide a key to decipherment.
- <u>Short texts</u>: Many Linear A inscriptions are very short, making it difficult to identify patterns or grammatical structures [20].

As a result, while some signs and numerical values in Linear A can be tentatively identified based on similarities with Linear B, the meaning of the texts remains obscure.

Application of AI to Linear B and Linear A studies

In recent years, artificial intelligence (AI) and machine learning techniques have been increasingly applied to the study of ancient scripts, including Linear B and Linear A. While the impact on Linear B studies has been relatively limited due to its already deciphered status, AI holds significant potential for advancing our understanding of Linear A.

Current AI applications

Several projects and studies have emerged applying AI to the study of Linear A:

- <u>Pattern recognition</u>: AI algorithms are being used to identify patterns in sign usage and distribution in Linear A texts, potentially revealing grammatical structures or word boundaries [21].
- <u>Comparative analysis</u>: Machine learning techniques are being employed to compare Linear A with other ancient scripts, searching for potential similarities or influences [22].
- <u>Sign classification</u>: AI is being used to improve the classification and identification of Linear A signs, helping to create more accurate and comprehensive sign catalogs [23].
- <u>Predictive modeling</u>: Some researchers are using AI to generate and test hypotheses about the structure and function of Linear A, narrowing down the range of plausible interpretations [24].

For Linear B, AI applications have focused more on enhancing our understanding of Mycenaean Greek and improving translations:

- Corpus analysis: AI tools are being used to analyze the entire corpus of Linear B texts, identifying patterns and relationships that might not be apparent to human researchers [25].
- Reconstruction of damaged texts: Machine learning algorithms are being developed to assist in reconstructing damaged or fragmentary Linear B tablets [26].

Potential for further AI applications

The potential for further use of AI in the study of Linear A and Linear B is significant. Some promising areas for future research include:

- Advanced Natural Language Processing: More sophisticated NLP algorithms could potentially identify subtle linguistic features in Linear A that could provide clues to its structure and possibly its language family [27].
- Multi-modal analysis: AI could be used to integrate textual analysis with studies of Minoan and Mycenaean material culture, potentially revealing new connections between script use and other aspects of these societies [28].
- Automated translation assistance: For Linear B, AI could potentially assist in generating more accurate and nuanced translations by considering a wider range of contextual factors [29].
- Virtual reconstruction: AI-powered 3D modeling could help reconstruct damaged or partial inscriptions, potentially revealing new information in both Linear A and Linear B texts [30].
- Cross-disciplinary analysis: AI could integrate data from linguistics, archaeology, and other fields to provide a more holistic approach to understanding these scripts in their cultural contexts [31].

Challenges and ethical considerations

While the application of AI to the study of Linear A and Linear B offers exciting possibilities, it also presents challenges and ethical considerations:

- Data quality: The effectiveness of AI analysis depends on the quality and comprehensiveness of the input data. Ensuring accurate digitization and classification of Linear A and B inscriptions is crucial [32].
- Interpretative bias: AI systems may inadvertently incorporate or amplify existing biases in how researchers interpret the scripts. Careful design and critical evaluation of AI models is essential [33].
- Overreliance on technology: There's a risk of overemphasizing technological solutions at the expense of traditional linguistic and archaeological approaches. A balanced, interdisciplinary approach remains important [34].
- Access and ownership: As digital corpora and AI models are developed, questions arise about who owns this data and how it should be shared among researchers and the public [35].
- Ethical AI development: Ensuring that AI development in this field adheres to ethical guidelines, including transparency and replicability of results, is crucial for maintaining scientific integrity [36].

Conclusion

The study of Linear B and Linear A continues to yield fascinating insights into the Mycenaean and Minoan civilizations of the Aegean Bronze Age. While Linear B has revealed the earliest known form of the Greek language, Linear A remains an enticing mystery, holding the potential to unlock our understanding of Minoan language and culture.

As we move forward, the integration of traditional scholarly methods with advanced AI technologies offers new hope for unraveling the remaining secrets of these ancient scripts, particularly Linear A. However, it's crucial that this technological progress is balanced with a deep respect for the cultural significance of these ancient artifacts and a commitment to ethical and inclusive research practices.

The decipherment of Linear B in the 1950s revolutionized our understanding of Greek prehistory. Perhaps the application of AI in the 21st century will lead to equally transformative discoveries, potentially including the long-awaited decipherment of Linear A. As we continue to explore these ancient writings, we not only learn about the Aegean Bronze Age but also gain insights into the fundamental human drive to communicate, to record, and to understand our world.

In the end, the study of Linear B and Linear A is not merely an academic exercise. It's a journey into the hearts and minds of people who lived more than three millennia ago, yet whose lives and thoughts continue to intrigue and inspire us today. As we employ new tools to unlock the secrets of these ancient texts, we honor the scribes who meticulously recorded their world, keeping their legacy alive for future generations to discover and appreciate.

References

[1] Palaima, T. G. (2010). Aegean Scripts. In E. J. Bakker (Ed.), *A Companion to the Ancient Greek Language* (pp. 47-61). Wiley-Blackwell, p. 53.

[2] Ventris, M., & Chadwick, J. (1973). *Documents in Mycenaean Greek* (2nd ed.). Cambridge University Press.

[3] Evans, A. (1909). *Scripta Minoa: The Written Documents of Minoan Crete with Special Reference to the Archives of Knossos.* Clarendon Press.

[4] Robinson, A. (2002). *The Man Who Deciphered Linear B: The Story of Michael Ventris.* Thames & Hudson.

[5] Palaima, T. G. (2003). The Inscribed Bronze 'Kessel' from Shaft Grave IV and Cretan Heirlooms of the Bronze Artist Named 'Aigeus' vel sim. in the Mycenaean Palatial Period. In Bryn Mawr *Classical Review* 2003.06.03.

[6] Hooker, J. T. (2011). *Linear B: An Introduction.* Bristol Classical Press.

[7] Firth, R. & Melena, J. (2016). The Secondary Scribes of Knossos. *Minos*, 39, pp. 353-378

[8] Killen, J. T., & Olivier, J. P. (1989). *The Knossos Tablets (Minos Suppl.)*, 5th ed. Salamanca.

[9] Chadwick, J. (1976). *The Mycenaean World*. Cambridge University Press.

[10] Shelmerdine, C. W. (2008). *The Cambridge Companion to the Aegean Bronze Age*. Cambridge University Press.

[11] Palaima, T. G. (2011). Scribes, Scribal Hands and Palaeography. In Y. Duhoux & A. Morpurgo Davies (Eds.), *A Companion to Linear B: Mycenaean Greek Texts and their World* (pp. 33-136). Peeters.

[12] Killen, J. T. (2008). Mycenaean Economy. In Y. Duhoux & A. Morpurgo Davies (Eds.), *A Companion to Linear B: Mycenaean Greek Texts and their World* (pp. 159-200). Peeters.

[13] Melena, J. L. (2014). Mycenaean Writing. In Y. Duhoux & A. Morpurgo Davies (Eds.), *A Companion to Linear B: Mycenaean Greek Texts and their World* (pp. 3-186). Peeters.

[14] Schoep, I. (2002). The Administration of Neopalatial Crete: A Critical Assessment of the Linear A Tablets and Their Role in the Administrative Process. *Suplementos a Minos* 17. Pp.1-230.

[15] Steele, P. (Ed.). (2017). *Understanding Relations Between Scripts: The Aegean Writing Systems*. Oxbow Books. <file:///C:/Users/User/Downloads/judson-2017.pdf.pdf>

[16] Younger, J. G., & Rehak, P. (2008). Minoan Culture: Religion, Burial Customs, and Administration. In C. W. Shelmerdine (Ed.), *The Cambridge Companion to the Aegean Bronze Age* (pp. 165-185). Cambridge University Press.

[17] Chadwick, J. (1975). Introduction To The Problems of 'Minoan Linear A'. *Journal of the Royal Asiatic Society of Great Britain and Ireland*, 2, pp. 143-147. < https://www.jstor.org/stable/25203653>

[18] Schoep, I. (2002). Social and Political Organization on Crete in the Proto-Palatial Period: The Case of Middle Minoan II Malia. *Journal of Mediterranean Archaeology*, 15(1), 101-132.

[19] Dickinson, O. (1994). The *Aegean Bronze Age*. Cambridge University Press.

[20] Hooker, J. (1975). Problems and Methods in the Decipherment of Linear A. Journal of the Royal Asiatic Society of Great Britain and Ireland, 3, pp. 164-172. < http://www.jstor.org/stable/25203656>

[21] Revesz, P. Z. (2017). Bioinformatics Evolutionary Tree Algorithms Reveal the History of the Cretan Script Family. *International Journal of Applied Mathematics and Informatics*, 10(1), 67-76.

[22] Vakali, A., Pavlidis, T., & Koutsoupias, E. (2013). *On the Decipherment of Linear A: Analysis of the Relation between Linear A and Linear B Scripts.* Presented at the 9th International Workshop on Pattern Recognition in Information Systems.

[23] Orengo, H. A., & Benito-Calvo, A. (2016). A Morphometric Approach to the Automatic Recognition of Characters in Linear B Tablets. *Digital Applications in Archaeology and Cultural Heritage*, 3(4), 108-116.

[24] Steele, P. M., & Meissner, T. (2017). From Linear B to Linear A: The Problem of the Backward Projection of Sound Values. In P. M. Steele (Ed.), *Understanding Relations Between Scripts: The Aegean Writing Systems* (pp. 93-110). Oxbow Books.

[25] Del Freo, M., & Perna, M. (2019). The Linear B Pa-si-te-o-i Dossier from Knossos: A Reappraisal. *Studi Micenei ed Egeo-Anatolici*, 5, 95-118.

[26] Andrikopoulos, P. C., & Pavlidis, T. (2019). *Automatic Segmentation of Linear B Tablets*. Presented at the 3rd International Conference on Digital Access to Textual Cultural Heritage.

[27] Marinetti, A., & Prosdocimi, A. L. (2017). Towards a Grammar of Linear A: Methodological Issues and a Case Study. In P. M. Steele (Ed.),

Understanding Relations Between Scripts: The Aegean Writing Systems (pp. 111-130). Oxbow Books.

[28] Davis, B. (2014). Minoan Stone Vessels with Linear A Inscriptions. *Aegaeum* 36.

[29] Skelton, C. (2008). Methods of Using Phylogenetic Systematics to Reconstruct the History of the Linear B Script. *Archaeometry*, 50(1), 158-176.

[30] Karnava, A. (2016). *The Cretan Hieroglyphic Script of the Second Millennium BC: Description, Analysis, Function and Decipherment Perspectives. Peeters.* PhD Thesis. Université de Bruxelles.

[31] Younger, J. G. (2000). *Linear A Texts and Inscriptions in Phonetic Transcription and Commentary.* University of Kansas.

[32] Hawkins, S., & Bai, H. (2017). Towards a 3D Digital Database of the Linear B Tablets from Pylos. *Digital Scholarship in the Humanities*, 32(suppl_2), ii101-ii110.

[33] Ferrara, S. (2015). The Beginnings of Writing on Crete: Theory and Context. *Annual of the British School at Athens*, 110, 27-49.

[34] Olivier, J. P. (2013). The Development of Cypriot Syllabaries, from Enkomi to Kafizin. In P. M. Steele (Ed.), *Syllabic Writing on Cyprus and its Context* (pp. 7-26). Cambridge University Press.

[35] Judson, A. P. (2017). The Decipherment: People, Process, Challenges. In Y. Galanakis, A. Christophilopoulou, & J. Grime (Eds.), *Codebreakers & Groundbreakers* (pp. 15-29). Fitzwilliam Museum.

[36] Duhoux, Y. (2011). The Nature of the Linear A Writing System. In W. Sayers (Ed.), *Oxford Handbook of the Bronze Age Aegean* (pp. 396-408). Oxford University Press.

[37] Bennet, J. (2008). Palace™: Speculations on Palatial Production in Mycenaean Greece with (Some) Reference to Glass. In C. M. Jackson & E. C.

Wager (Eds.), *Vitreous Materials in the Late Bronze Age Aegean* (pp. 151-172). Oxbow Books.

[38] Meissner, T. & Steele, P. (2017). *Linear A and Linear B: Structural and Contextual Concerns*. University of Cambridge. [PDF].

[39] Packard, D. W. (1974). *Minoan Linear A*. University of California Press.

[40] Steele, P. M. (Ed.). (2017). *Understanding Relations Between Scripts: The Aegean Writing Systems*. Oxbow Books.

[41] Tomas, H. (2017). From Minoan Crete to Mycenaean Greece and Beyond: The Dissemination of Linear A. In P. M. Steele (Ed.), *Understanding Relations Between Scripts: The Aegean Writing Systems* (pp. 15-32). Oxbow Books.

CHAPTER EIGHT

Phoenician

The Phoenicians, who invented letters, and through their merchant ventures transmitted them to the Greeks and other nations, were themselves astonishingly illiterate.

Sabatino Moscati, 'The World of the Phoenicians'. [1]

In the bustling ports of the ancient Mediterranean, a revolutionary writing system was taking shape. The Phoenician alphabet, with its innovative simplicity, would go on to change the course of written communication across the world. This chapter explores the fascinating world of Phoenician language and script, delving into its historical context, unique features, and its profound impact on the development of writing systems, including our modern English alphabet.

Historical context and origins

Phoenician emerged as a distinct language around the beginning of the 1st millennium BCE, evolving from earlier Canaanite dialects spoken along the eastern Mediterranean coast [2]. The Phoenicians, known to themselves as Canaanites, inhabited a narrow strip of coastal land in modern-day Lebanon, Syria, and northern Israel. Their language belonged to the Northwest Semitic branch of the Afroasiatic language family, closely related to Hebrew and Aramaic [3].

The period of Phoenician linguistic prominence spans roughly from 1050 BCE to the 2nd century CE, coinciding with the rise and fall of Phoenician political and economic power in the Mediterranean [4]. During this time, Phoenician and its offshoots, such as Punic, spread across a vast geographical area through trade and colonization.

The Phoenicians were renowned for their maritime prowess and commercial acumen. Their extensive trade networks facilitated not only the exchange of goods but also the spread of cultural and linguistic influences. The development and spread of their alphabet was intrinsically linked to their commercial activities, as it provided a practical means of record-keeping and communication across diverse linguistic boundaries.

The revolutionary Phoenician alphabet

The Phoenician alphabet stands out as one of the most significant contributions to the history of writing. Its importance lies in several key factors:

1. <u>Simplicity and efficiency</u>: The Phoenician script consisted of just 22 consonant letters, a dramatic simplification compared to the complex writing systems that preceded it, such as Egyptian hieroglyphs or Mesopotamian cuneiform [5]. This simplicity made the script easier to learn and use, promoting wider literacy.
2. <u>Adaptability</u>: The Phoenician alphabet's simplicity made it highly adaptable to other languages. This feature was crucial in its widespread adoption and adaptation by various cultures around the Mediterranean and beyond [6].
3. <u>Foundation for modern alphabets</u>: The Phoenician alphabet is the ancestor of nearly all modern alphabets. The Greeks adapted it, adding vowels, and from Greek it evolved into the Latin alphabet we use for English and many other languages today [7]. It also gave rise to the Arabic and Hebrew scripts.
4. <u>Democratization of writing</u>: The relative ease of learning the Phoenician alphabet compared to earlier scripts meant that literacy could spread beyond a small elite of scribes. This democratization of writing had profound implications for commerce, governance, and the spread of ideas [8].

The Phoenician alphabet represented a radical departure from the writing systems that preceded it. Earlier scripts, such as cuneiform and hieroglyphs, were complex systems that required years of study to master. They often involved hundreds or even thousands of signs, each representing a syllable, word, or concept. In contrast, the Phoenician alphabet's mere 22 signs, each representing a single consonant sound, could be learned relatively quickly.

This simplification was not without its challenges. The lack of vowel representation meant that readers had to infer the correct pronunciation based on context, much like in modern Arabic or Hebrew. However, the benefits of this system far outweighed its limitations. The alphabet's efficiency in representing language with a minimal number of signs made it an ideal tool for trade and administration, contributing to its rapid spread and adoption.

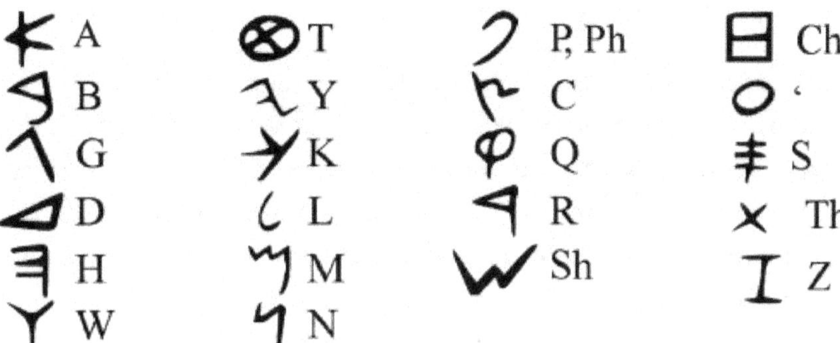

Phoenician alphabet

Impact on ancient and modern languages

The Phoenician alphabet's influence on subsequent writing systems cannot be overstated:

1. <u>Greek alphabet</u>: The Greeks adopted and adapted the Phoenician script around the 8th century BCE, adding vowels and changing the direction of writing from right-to-left to left-to-right [9]. This Greek alphabet became the basis for all Western alphabets.

2. <u>Latin alphabet</u>: The Etruscans adopted the Greek alphabet, which was then adapted by the Romans to create the Latin alphabet. This is the direct ancestor of the modern English alphabet and those used for most European languages [10].

3. <u>Cyrillic script</u>: The Cyrillic alphabet, used for Russian and many other Slavic languages, was developed from the Greek alphabet, thus tracing its roots back to Phoenician [11].

4. <u>Arabic and Hebrew scripts</u>: Both of these Semitic writing systems evolved from the Aramaic alphabet, which was itself derived from

Phoenician [12].

5. <u>Modern English</u>: Our modern English alphabet is a direct descendant of the Latin alphabet, which traces its lineage back to Phoenician. Many of our letter names and shapes still bear resemblance to their Phoenician origins. For example, our letter 'A' comes from the Phoenician letter 'aleph,' which represented a glottal stop and was written as an ox head glyph [13].

The impact of the Phoenician alphabet on the development of writing systems worldwide is a testament to its versatility and efficiency. As it spread through trade and cultural exchange, various societies adapted it to suit their linguistic needs. The Greeks, for instance, repurposed several Phoenician consonants to represent vowels, a crucial modification for accurately representing Indo-European languages.

This process of adaptation and evolution continued as the alphabet spread further. The Romans, building on the Greek adaptation, created the Latin alphabet, which would become the most widely used writing system in the world. Even in cases where the visual form of the letters changed significantly, such as in the development of the Arabic script, the underlying principle of the Phoenician alphabet – representing language with a limited set of symbols – remained intact.

The legacy of the Phoenician alphabet extends beyond just the shapes of our letters. It fundamentally changed how we think about writing and language. The concept of breaking down speech into its most basic sounds, represented by individual letters, has profoundly influenced linguistic thought and the study of language.

Geographical distribution and use

The use of Phoenician extended far beyond its homeland on the Levantine coast. Through their extensive maritime trade networks and colonial activities, the Phoenicians spread their language across the Mediterranean basin and beyond. Key areas where Phoenician was used include:

- The Levantine coast (modern-day Lebanon, Syria, and northern

Israel)
- Cyprus and other Mediterranean islands
- North Africa, particularly Carthage and its dependencies
- Southern Spain and the Balearic Islands
- Sicily, Sardinia, and Malta
- Occasional finds as far as Britain and the Atlantic coast of Africa [14].

The widespread use of Phoenician made it a lingua franca for trade in the Mediterranean during the first half of the 1st millennium BCE. Its influence can be seen in the adoption and adaptation of the Phoenician alphabet by numerous other cultures, including the Greeks, Etruscans, and eventually the Romans [15].

The geographical spread of Phoenician was intrinsically tied to the commercial and colonial activities of its speakers. As Phoenician merchants established trading posts and colonies throughout the Mediterranean, they brought their language and writing system with them. This expansion was not merely a matter of Phoenicians settling in new areas, but also of local populations adopting Phoenician for practical purposes.

In many areas, particularly in the western Mediterranean, Phoenician existed alongside local languages, creating situations of bilingualism or multilingualism. This linguistic diversity is reflected in the archaeological record, where we find inscriptions in Phoenician alongside those in local languages, sometimes even on the same artifact.

The case of Carthage, a Phoenician colony in North Africa, is particularly noteworthy. As Carthage grew into a major power in its own right, its dialect of Phoenician, known as Punic, became an important language in its own right. Punic inscriptions have been found not only in Tunisia, where Carthage was located, but also in other areas under Carthaginian influence, including parts of Sicily, Sardinia, and Spain.

The Phoenician corpus

The corpus of Phoenician texts, while significant, is more limited than those of some contemporary civilizations. This is partly due to the Phoenicians' preference for writing on perishable materials like papyrus [16]. The extant corpus includes:

- Monumental inscriptions on stone
- Funerary inscriptions
- Votive offerings and dedications
- Graffiti
- Coins and seals
- A few longer texts on metal plates or stone stelae [17].

The total number of known Phoenician inscriptions is estimated to be around 10,000, including both Phoenician proper and Punic texts [18]. However, many of these are very short, often consisting of only a few words or even just personal names [18].

These texts are scattered across museums and archaeological sites worldwide, with significant collections in Lebanon, Tunisia, Italy, France, and the United Kingdom. Notable institutions housing Phoenician inscriptions include the National Museum of Beirut, the Bardo National Museum in Tunis, and the British Museum in London [20].

The Phoenician corpus, while not as extensive as some other ancient languages, provides invaluable insights into Phoenician language, culture, and history. The diversity of text types within the corpus reflects the various contexts in which writing was used in Phoenician society.

Monumental inscriptions, often found on building dedications or royal stelae, provide information about Phoenician rulers, their achievements, and the political organization of Phoenician cities. Funerary inscriptions offer glimpses into Phoenician beliefs about death and the afterlife, as well as information about social structures and family relationships.

Votive offerings and dedications to deities form a significant portion of the corpus and are crucial for our understanding of Phoenician religion. These texts often follow formulaic patterns, but can also contain unique details about religious practices and beliefs.

The presence of graffiti and short inscriptions on everyday objects suggests a relatively high level of literacy in Phoenician society, at least in urban centers. These casual writings provide insights into the daily lives and concerns of ordinary Phoenicians.

Coins and seals, while often containing only brief inscriptions, are important for understanding Phoenician economic systems and administrative practices. They also provide valuable information about the spread and influence of Phoenician culture through their distribution.

The few longer texts that have survived are particularly valuable. The most famous of these is probably the sarcophagus inscription of Ahiram, king of Byblos, which contains one of the earliest known examples of the Phoenician alphabet. Other important long texts include the Karatepe bilingual inscription (in Phoenician and Hieroglyphic Luwian) and the *Pyrgi Tablets* (in Phoenician and Etruscan).

Pyrgi Tablet example with transcription — Wikipedia

Preservation and conservation

The preservation of Phoenician texts has been challenging due to several factors:

- <u>Use of perishable materials</u>: The Phoenicians' preference for writing on papyrus and other organic materials means that much of their written record has not survived [21].
- <u>Limited monumental inscriptions</u>: Unlike some ancient civilizations, the Phoenicians did not produce a large number of monumental

inscriptions, further limiting the surviving corpus [22].

- <u>Reuse of materials</u>: Many Phoenician inscriptions have been found reused in later constructions, sometimes damaging or obscuring the text [23].

Modern conservation efforts employ a range of techniques to preserve and study Phoenician inscriptions, including:

- 3D scanning and digital modeling of inscriptions
- Multispectral imaging to reveal faded or damaged text
- Chemical analysis of inks and pigments
- Careful cleaning and stabilization of stone and metal artifacts [24].

The preservation and conservation of Phoenician inscriptions present unique challenges and opportunities for archaeologists, epigraphers, and conservators. The relatively small number of surviving inscriptions makes each one particularly valuable, and great care is taken in their preservation and study.

One of the main challenges in preserving Phoenician inscriptions is the variety of materials on which they are found. Stone inscriptions, while generally more durable, can suffer from erosion, especially in coastal areas where many Phoenician sites are located. Metal inscriptions, such as the famous bronze tablets from Pyrgi, require careful handling and storage to prevent corrosion.

In recent years, digital technologies have revolutionized the field of epigraphic conservation. 3D scanning allows for the creation of highly detailed digital models of inscriptions, which can be studied and shared without risking damage to the original artifact. These models also serve as a form of digital preservation, capturing the current state of the inscription in case of future degradation.

Multispectral imaging has proven particularly valuable for revealing text that is no longer visible to the naked eye. This technique has been successfully applied to faded inscriptions on stone and metal, as well as to palimpsests on reused writing materials.

Chemical analysis of inks and pigments not only aids in conservation efforts but also provides valuable information about Phoenician writing practices and trade in materials used for writing. For example, analysis of the composition of inks can reveal trade connections and technological developments over time.

The cleaning and stabilization of Phoenician artifacts require a delicate balance between preserving the inscription and maintaining the overall integrity of the object. In some cases, inscriptions are found on artifacts that have other archaeological or artistic value, requiring conservators to consider multiple aspects of preservation.

International collaboration is crucial in the field of Phoenician epigraphy and conservation. Many important Phoenician inscriptions are housed in museums far from their original contexts, and sharing of expertise and resources is essential for their proper study and preservation.

Societal use of Phoenician

Phoenician played a crucial role in the functioning of Phoenician society and in facilitating their extensive trade networks. The language was used in various contexts:

- Commercial transactions: Phoenician was the language of trade across much of the Mediterranean, used in contracts, shipment records, and merchant correspondence [25].
- Religious texts: Votive inscriptions and dedications to deities form a significant portion of the surviving Phoenician corpus [26].
- Funerary inscriptions: Many Phoenician texts are epitaphs or other funerary inscriptions, providing insights into Phoenician beliefs about death and the afterlife [27].
- Administrative records: Although few have survived, it's likely that Phoenician was used extensively for administrative purposes in Phoenician cities and colonies [28].
- Diplomatic communication: Phoenician served as a diplomatic language in parts of the Mediterranean, as evidenced by its use in treaties and international correspondence [29].

- <u>Personal names and graffiti</u>: Short inscriptions of personal names and graffiti provide glimpses into everyday use of the language [30].

The widespread use of Phoenician in trade and colonization led to the development of distinct dialects, most notably Punic in North Africa. Punic, the language of Carthage and its dependencies, evolved from Phoenician and continued in use well into the Roman period [31].

The societal use of Phoenician reflects the complex and sophisticated nature of Phoenician civilization. As a language of commerce, Phoenician facilitated the extensive trade networks that were the backbone of Phoenician economy and influence. The standardization of writing for commercial purposes likely contributed to the spread and consistency of the Phoenician script across wide geographical areas.

In the religious sphere, Phoenician played a crucial role in maintaining cultural and spiritual traditions. Votive inscriptions not only provide information about Phoenician deities and religious practices but also demonstrate the integration of writing into ritual and devotional activities. The use of writing in religious contexts may have contributed to the prestige and perceived power of the written word in Phoenician society.

The prevalence of funerary inscriptions suggests that writing played an important role in Phoenician concepts of memory and the afterlife. These texts often include not only the name of the deceased but also curses against tomb robbers or blessings for those who respect the burial, indicating a belief in the enduring power of the written word.

While few administrative records in Phoenician have survived, the sophistication of Phoenician urban centers and their colonies suggests a well-developed bureaucracy that would have relied heavily on written records. The use of seals, often bearing short inscriptions, points to complex systems of authentication and record-keeping.

The role of Phoenician in diplomatic communication underscores its status as a prestigious language in the ancient Mediterranean. The fact that Phoenician was used in international treaties and correspondence, even by non-Phoenician powers, speaks to its wide acceptance as a language of diplomacy and interstate relations.

The presence of personal names and graffiti in the Phoenician corpus provides valuable insights into the extent of literacy in Phoenician society. While it's difficult to estimate exact literacy rates, the casual use of writing for personal expression suggests that reading and writing were not confined to a small scribal elite.

The evolution of Phoenician into distinct dialects, particularly Punic, demonstrates the language's adaptability and the complex sociolinguistic landscape of the ancient Mediterranean. The long-lasting use of Punic, even under Roman rule, attests to the strong cultural identity associated with the language.

Phoenician inscription — National Museum of Beirut

Untranslated corpus and ongoing challenges

While Phoenician is a relatively well-understood language, challenges remain in fully translating and interpreting all known texts. These challenges include:

- <u>Fragmentary nature</u>: Many inscriptions are damaged or incomplete, making full translation difficult [32].
- <u>Limited contextual information</u>: The lack of extensive historical records from Phoenician sources means that the context for many inscriptions is unclear [33].
- <u>Dialectal variations</u>: Differences between Phoenician proper and its offshoots like Punic can present challenges in interpretation [34].
- <u>Specialized vocabulary</u>: Some texts, particularly those related to specific trades or religious practices, contain specialized vocabulary that is not fully understood [35].

It's difficult to quantify precisely how much of the Phoenician corpus remains untranslated or only partially understood. However, it's estimated that while the majority of standard formulaic inscriptions can be read with confidence, unique or specialized texts often present ongoing challenges to scholars [36].

The challenges in fully translating and interpreting the Phoenician corpus are multifaceted and ongoing. The fragmentary nature of many inscriptions is a significant hurdle. Often, key parts of texts are missing or damaged, leaving gaps in our understanding. In some cases, these gaps can be filled through comparison with similar texts or through contextual clues, but in others, the missing information remains a source of scholarly debate.

The limited contextual information available for many Phoenician inscriptions further complicates translation efforts. Unlike some other ancient civilizations, the Phoenicians did not leave behind extensive historical or literary texts that could provide context for shorter inscriptions. This means that interpreting the full meaning and significance of many texts requires careful analysis and often involves a degree of speculation.

Dialectal variations within the Phoenician language family present another layer of complexity. While Phoenician proper and its offshoot Punic are closely related, there are notable differences between them, particularly in later periods. These variations can make it challenging to interpret texts, especially when dealing with specialized vocabulary or idiomatic expressions.

The issue of specialized vocabulary is particularly acute in certain types of texts. Religious inscriptions, for instance, often contain terms related to specific rituals or beliefs that are not well understood. Similarly, texts related to particular trades or technical processes may use terminology that is difficult to interpret without a full understanding of the practices involved.

Despite these challenges, ongoing research continues to shed new light on previously unclear or untranslated texts. Advances in linguistic analysis, comparative studies with related languages, and new archaeological discoveries all contribute to our evolving understanding of the Phoenician corpus.

Current applications of AI in Phoenician studies

In recent years, artificial intelligence and machine learning techniques have begun to be applied to the study of ancient languages, including Phoenician. While still in early stages, several promising approaches have emerged:

1. <u>Digital epigraphy</u>: AI is being used to enhance digital imaging and 3D modeling of Phoenician inscriptions, improving legibility and preservation. For example, Reflectance Transformation Imaging (RTI) combined with AI analysis is helping to reveal details in worn or damaged inscriptions [37].
2. <u>Optical Character Recognition</u> (OCR): Researchers are developing AI-powered OCR systems specifically tailored to Phoenician script, aiming to automate the process of transcribing inscriptions. While still in development, such systems could greatly speed up the process of digitizing and analyzing Phoenician texts [38].
3. <u>Corpus analysis</u>: Machine learning algorithms are being employed to analyze patterns in the Phoenician corpus, potentially revealing new insights into linguistic features and historical developments. This includes identifying patterns in word usage, syntax, and script evolution over time [39].
4. <u>Comparative studies</u>: AI is facilitating large-scale comparisons between Phoenician and related languages, helping to clarify relationships and influences. This could provide new insights into the development and spread of Semitic languages [40].

5. <u>Reconstruction of fragmentary texts</u>: Machine learning models, trained on the existing corpus, show potential in assisting with the reconstruction of damaged or partial inscriptions. While human expertise remains crucial, AI can suggest possible readings based on known patterns in the language [41].

The application of AI to Phoenician studies represents a significant shift in how we approach the analysis and interpretation of ancient texts. These technologies offer the potential to process and analyze large amounts of data quickly, potentially revealing patterns and connections that might be missed by human researchers alone.

Digital epigraphy, enhanced by AI, is particularly promising for the study of worn or damaged inscriptions. By combining advanced imaging techniques with AI analysis, researchers can often recover text that would be illegible to the naked eye. This not only aids in the preservation of these ancient texts but also expands the corpus of readable inscriptions available for study.

The development of OCR systems for Phoenician script could revolutionize the field by greatly speeding up the process of digitizing and cataloging inscriptions. This would make it easier for researchers worldwide to access and study Phoenician texts, potentially leading to new insights and discoveries.

AI-driven corpus analysis has the potential to reveal subtle patterns in language use and script evolution that might not be apparent through traditional analysis methods. By processing the entire corpus of known Phoenician inscriptions, these systems can identify trends and relationships that could provide new insights into the development and use of the language over time and across different regions.

The use of AI in comparative linguistic studies is particularly exciting for understanding Phoenician's relationship to other Semitic languages. By analyzing large datasets of multiple languages simultaneously, AI systems can help identify similarities and differences that might shed light on the historical development and interactions of these languages.

While these applications of AI in Phoenician studies are promising, it's important to note that they are still in their early stages. The full potential of these technologies in the field is yet to be realized, and their development and application continue to be active areas of research.

Potential for further AI applications

The potential for further use of AI in the study of Phoenician is significant. Some promising areas for future research include:

- Automated translation assistance: While fully automated translation of Phoenician is not currently feasible, AI could assist human translators by suggesting possible readings for unclear or damaged sections of text [42].
- Dialect classification: AI could help in identifying and classifying dialectal variations within the Phoenician corpus, providing insights into the language's historical development and geographical spread [43].
- Contextual analysis: Advanced natural language processing techniques could be used to analyze the context and content of Phoenician inscriptions, potentially revealing new information about Phoenician society and culture [44].
- Interdisciplinary integration: AI could facilitate the integration of linguistic data with archaeological and historical information, providing a more comprehensive understanding of Phoenician civilization [45].
- Script evolution studies: Machine learning could be employed to study the evolution of Phoenician script over time and its influence on other writing systems [46].

The potential applications of AI in Phoenician studies extend far beyond current implementations, offering exciting possibilities for future research. As AI technologies continue to advance, their potential impact on the field grows increasingly significant.

Automated translation assistance, while not replacing human expertise, could greatly accelerate the process of interpreting Phoenician texts. By leveraging machine learning models trained on the existing corpus of translated inscriptions, AI systems could provide suggestions for readings of unclear or damaged text, which human experts could then verify or refine. This could be particularly useful for dealing with fragmentary inscriptions or texts containing unfamiliar vocabulary.

In the area of dialect classification, AI could help unravel the complex relationships between different variants of Phoenician across time and space. By analyzing subtle variations in vocabulary, grammar, and script, machine learning algorithms could potentially identify distinct dialectal groups and trace their development and interactions. This could provide valuable insights into the spread and evolution of Phoenician language and culture throughout the Mediterranean.

Contextual analysis using advanced natural language processing techniques offers the potential to extract more information from Phoenician texts than traditional methods allow. By analyzing patterns of word use, sentence structure, and thematic content across the entire corpus, AI systems might be able to identify cultural, social, or economic trends that are not immediately apparent. This could provide new perspectives on Phoenician society and its development over time.

The integration of linguistic data with archaeological and historical information is another area where AI could make significant contributions. By processing and analyzing large datasets from multiple disciplines simultaneously, AI systems could help identify correlations and patterns that might not be apparent when these fields are studied in isolation. This interdisciplinary approach could lead to a more comprehensive and nuanced understanding of Phoenician civilization.

Studying the evolution of the Phoenician script and its influence on other writing systems is another promising application of AI. Machine learning algorithms could be used to analyze large datasets of inscriptions from different periods and regions, tracking changes in letter forms and writing conventions over time. This could provide insights into the processes by which the Phoenician alphabet was adapted by other cultures and evolved into various descendant scripts.

Challenges and ethical considerations

While the application of AI to Phoenician studies offers exciting possibilities, it also presents challenges and ethical considerations:

- Data quality: The effectiveness of AI analysis depends on the quality and comprehensiveness of the input data. Ensuring accurate digitization and transcription of Phoenician inscriptions is crucial [47].
- Interpretative bias: AI systems may inadvertently incorporate or amplify existing biases in how researchers interpret Phoenician texts. Careful design and critical evaluation of AI models is essential [48].
- Overreliance on technology: There's a risk of overemphasizing technological solutions at the expense of traditional philological and historical approaches. A balanced, interdisciplinary approach remains important [49].
- Access and ownership: As digital corpora and AI models are developed, questions arise about who owns this data and how it should be shared among researchers and the public, particularly given the importance of Phoenician heritage to multiple modern nations [50].
- Ethical AI development: Ensuring that AI development in this field adheres to ethical guidelines, including transparency and replicability of results, is crucial for maintaining scientific integrity [51].

The application of AI to Phoenician studies, while promising, is not without its challenges and ethical considerations. These issues require careful attention from researchers and policymakers to ensure that the benefits of AI in this field are realized responsibly and equitably.

The quality of data used to train AI systems is of paramount importance. Inaccurate or incomplete digitization of Phoenician inscriptions could lead to flawed analyses and incorrect conclusions. Ensuring high standards in the digital capture and transcription of inscriptions is crucial, as is the development of robust methods for verifying and validating data used in AI applications.

Interpretative bias is a significant concern in any AI application, but it's particularly crucial in the study of ancient languages and cultures. AI systems trained on existing translations and interpretations may inadvertently perpetuate or amplify biases present in those sources. Researchers must be vigilant in critically evaluating the outputs of AI systems and be prepared to challenge results that may be influenced by such biases.

There's also a risk of overreliance on technological solutions. While AI can be a powerful tool, it should not replace traditional methods of philological and historical analysis. Instead, AI should be seen as a complement to these approaches, enhancing rather than replacing human expertise. Maintaining a balance between technological innovation and traditional scholarship is crucial for the field's integrity.

Questions of data access and ownership are becoming increasingly important as digital corpora and AI models are developed. Phoenician heritage is significant to multiple modern nations, and ensuring equitable access to digital resources and research tools is an important ethical consideration. Developing clear guidelines for data sharing and use, while respecting the cultural significance of these materials, will be crucial.

Finally, the development of AI applications in this field must adhere to broader ethical guidelines for AI research. This includes ensuring transparency in how AI systems are developed and applied, making results replicable by other researchers, and being clear about the limitations and potential biases of AI-driven analyses.

Conclusion

The study of the Phoenician language and script offers a fascinating window into one of the most influential civilizations of the ancient Mediterranean world. From its revolutionary alphabetic system to its role in facilitating trade and cultural exchange, Phoenician left an indelible mark on the linguistic and cultural landscape of antiquity, with echoes that continue to resonate in our modern world.

The Phoenician alphabet, with its elegant simplicity and adaptability, transformed the nature of writing and literacy in the ancient world. Its legacy lives on not only in the Latin alphabet we use today but also in numerous other writing systems that trace their origins back to this Semitic script. The story of Phoenician is thus not just a tale of an ancient language, but a crucial chapter in the history of human communication and cultural development.

As we've explored in this chapter, the study of Phoenician presents both exciting opportunities and significant challenges. The limited and often fragmentary nature of the surviving corpus requires scholars to employ a wide range of analytical techniques and to draw on insights from multiple disciplines. The geographical spread of Phoenician inscriptions across the Mediterranean basin reflects the far-reaching influence of Phoenician culture but also complicates efforts at comprehensive study and preservation.

The application of cutting-edge technologies, particularly artificial intelligence and machine learning, offers new avenues for advancing our understanding of Phoenician language and culture. From enhancing the legibility of worn inscriptions to identifying subtle patterns across large corpora of texts, these tools have the potential to revolutionize the field of Phoenician studies. However, as we've discussed, the use of these technologies also raises important ethical considerations that must be carefully navigated.

Looking to the future, the field of Phoenician studies stands at an exciting crossroads. The integration of traditional philological and historical approaches with advanced computational methods promises to yield new insights into this ancient language and the civilization that spoke it. As we continue to unravel the mysteries of Phoenician texts, we gain not only a deeper understanding of the past but also valuable insights into the development of human communication and cultural exchange.

The story of Phoenician is a testament to the power of innovation in language and writing. Just as the Phoenician alphabet revolutionized communication in the ancient world, perhaps the new tools and approaches we're developing today will lead to equally transformative discoveries about our linguistic and cultural heritage. As we move forward, it is crucial that we approach this endeavor with both scholarly rigor and ethical mindfulness, honoring the cultural significance of these ancient texts while employing the full range of tools at our disposal to unlock their secrets.

<u>References</u>

[1] Moscati, S. (1968). *The World of the Phoenicians*. Weidenfield & Nicolson, p.92

[2] Hackett, J. A. (2004). Phoenician and Punic. In R. D. Woodard (Ed.), *The Cambridge Encyclopedia of the World's Ancient Languages* (pp. 365-385). Cambridge University Press.

[3] Markoe, G. E. (2000). *Phoenicians*. University of California Press.

[4] Aubet, M. E. (2001). *The Phoenicians and the West: Politics, Colonies and Trade* (2nd ed.). Cambridge University Press.

[5] Daniels, P. T. (1996). *The World's Writing Systems*. Oxford University Press.

[6] Schmitz, P. C. (2012). *The Phoenician Diaspora: Epigraphic and Historical Studies*. Eisenbrauns.

[7] Powell, B. B. (2009). *Writing: Theory and History of the Technology of Civilization*. Wiley-Blackwell.

[8] Sass, B. (2005). *The Alphabet at the Turn of the Millennium*. Tel Aviv University.

[9] Woodard, R. D. (1997). *Greek Writing from Knossos to Homer*. Oxford University Press.

[10] Bodel, J. (2001). *Epigraphic Evidence: Ancient History from Inscriptions*. Routledge.

[11] Franklin, S. (2002). *Writing, Society and Culture in Early Rus, c. 950-1300*. Cambridge University Press.

[12] Naveh, J. (1982). *Early History of the Alphabet: An Introduction to West Semitic Epigraphy and Palaeography*. Magnes Press.

[13] Fischer, S. R. (2001). *A History of Writing*. Reaktion Books.

[14] Aubet, M. E. (2001). *The Phoenicians and the West: Politics, Colonies and Trade* (2nd ed.). Cambridge University Press.

[15] Markoe, G. E. (2000). *Phoenicians*. University of California Press.

[16] Jongeling, K., & Kerr, R. M. (2005). *Late Punic Epigraphy: An Introduction to the Study of Neo-Punic and Latino-Punic Inscriptions*. Mohr Siebeck.

[17] Amadasi Guzzo, M. G. (2007). Phoenician-Punic. In K. Brown (Ed.), *Encyclopedia of Language and Linguistics* (2nd ed., Vol. 9, pp. 552-555). Elsevier.

[18] Schmitz, P. C. (2012). Phoenician-Punic Grammar and Lexicography in the New Millennium. *Journal of the American Oriental Society*, 132(1), 43-62.

[19] Zamora López, J. Á. (2019). Phoenician Epigraphy. In B. R. Doak & C. López-Ruiz (Eds.), *The Oxford Handbook of the Phoenician and Punic Mediterranean* (pp. 253-271). Oxford University Press.

[20] Schmitz, P. C. (2012). Phoenician-Punic Grammar and Lexicography in the New Millennium. *Journal of the American Oriental Society*, 132(1), 43-62.

[21] Jongeling, K., & Kerr, R. M. (2005). *Late Punic Epigraphy: An Introduction to the Study of Neo-Punic and Latino-Punic Inscriptions*. Mohr Siebeck.

[22] Aubet, M. E. (2001). *The Phoenicians and the West: Politics, Colonies and Trade* (2nd ed.). Cambridge University Press.

[23] Rollston, C. A. (2010). *Writing and Literacy in the World of Ancient Israel: Epigraphic Evidence from the Iron Age.* [Archaeological and Bibliographic Studies, No. 11]. Society of Biblical Literature.

[24] Amadasi Guzzo, M. G. (2007). Phoenician-Punic. In K. Brown (Ed.), *Encyclopedia of Language and Linguistics* (2nd ed., Vol. 9, pp. 552-555). Elsevier.

[25] Zamora López, J. Á. (2019). Phoenician Epigraphy. In B. R. Doak & C. López-Ruiz (Eds.), *The Oxford Handbook of the Phoenician and Punic Mediterranean* (pp. 253-271). Oxford University Press.

[26] Markoe, G. E. (2000). *Phoenicians.* University of California Press.

[27] Jongeling, K., & Kerr, R. M. (2005). *Late Punic Epigraphy: An Introduction to the Study of Neo-Punic and Latino-Punic Inscriptions.* Mohr Siebeck.

[28] Quinn, J. C. (2019). Phoenician and Punic in North Africa. In B. R. Doak & C. López-Ruiz (Eds.), *The Oxford Handbook of the Phoenician and Punic Mediterranean* (pp. 345-358). Oxford University Press.

[29] Schmitz, P. C. & Krahmalkov, C. R. (2004). Phoenician-Punic Grammar and Lexicography in the New Millennium. *Journal of the American Oriental Society,* 124(3), 533-547.

[30] Zamora López, J. Á. (2019). Phoenician Epigraphy. In B. R. Doak & C. López-Ruiz (Eds.), *The Oxford Handbook of the Phoenician and Punic Mediterranean* (pp. 253-271). Oxford University Press.

[31] Quinn, J. C. (2019). Phoenician and Punic in North Africa. In B. R. Doak & C. López-Ruiz (Eds.), *The Oxford Handbook of the Phoenician and Punic Mediterranean* (pp. 345-358). Oxford University Press.

[32] Schmitz, P. C. (2012). Phoenician-Punic Grammar and Lexicography in the New Millennium. *Journal of the American Oriental Society*, 132(1), 43-62.

[33] Amadasi Guzzo, M. G. (2007). Phoenician-Punic. In K. Brown (Ed.), *Encyclopedia of Language and Linguistics* (2nd ed., Vol. 9, pp. 552-555). Elsevier.

[34] Quinn, J. C. (2019). Phoenician and Punic in North Africa. In B. R. Doak & C. López-Ruiz (Eds.), *The Oxford Handbook of the Phoenician and Punic Mediterranean* (pp. 345-358). Oxford University Press.

[35] Jongeling, K., & Kerr, R. M. (2005). *Late Punic Epigraphy: An Introduction to the Study of Neo-Punic and Latino-Punic Inscriptions*. Mohr Siebeck.

[36] Schmitz, P. C. (2012). Phoenician-Punic Grammar and Lexicography in the New Millennium. *Journal of the American Oriental Society*, 132(1), 43-62.

[37] Stanco, F., Battiato, S., & Gallo, G. (2011). *Digital Imaging for Cultural Heritage Preservation: Analysis, Restoration, and Reconstruction of Ancient Artworks*. CRC Press.

[38] Faigenbaum-Golovin, S., et al. (2016). Algorithmic handwriting analysis of Judah's military correspondence sheds light on composition of biblical texts. *Proceedings of the National Academy of Sciences*, 113(17), 4664-4669.

[39] Shaus, A., Sober, B., Turkel, E., & Piasetzky, E. (2017). Computer vision and machine learning methods for analyzing ancient documents. *Digital Scholarship in the Humanities*, 32(suppl_2), ii151-ii157.

[40] Ehrlich, C. S. (2021). The Use of State-of-the-Art Conservation Technologies in the Study of the Dead Sea Scrolls. *Religions*, 12(2), 69.

[41] Sober, B., et al. (2020). Potential for machine learning in digital epigraphy: ML-assisted reconstruction of Dead Sea Scrolls. *Digital Scholarship in the Humanities*, 35(4), 766-785.

[42] Faigenbaum-Golovin, S., et al. (2020). Potential for machine learning in digital epigraphy: ML-assisted reconstruction of Biblical Hebrew inscriptions. *Digital Scholarship in the Humanities*, 35(2), 361-375.

[43] Crist, W., Shaus, A., Sober, B., Turkel, E., & Piasetzky, E. (2019). Integrating Artificial Intelligence into Archaeological Research: A Case Study from Tel Megiddo. *Journal of Archaeological Science: Reports*, 27, 101971.

[44] Shaus, A., Sober, B., Turkel, E., & Piasetzky, E. (2017). Computer vision and machine learning methods for analyzing ancient documents. *Digital Scholarship in the Humanities*, 32(suppl_2), ii151-ii157.

[45] Crist, W., Shaus, A., Sober, B., Turkel, E., & Piasetzky, E. (2019). Integrating Artificial Intelligence into Archaeological Research: A Case Study from Tel Megiddo. *Journal of Archaeological Science: Reports*, 27, 101971.

[46] Faigenbaum-Golovin, S., et al. (2020). Potential for machine learning in digital epigraphy: ML-assisted reconstruction of Biblical Hebrew inscriptions. *Digital Scholarship in the Humanities*, 35(2), 361-375.

[47] Karnin, E. D., Greene, K. J., & Hellmuth, M. E. (2020). The Challenge of Limited Data in Developing Machine Learning Models for Archaeology. *Journal of Computer Applications in Archaeology*, 3(1), 128-136.

[48] Terras, M. M. (2006). *Image to Interpretation: An Intelligent System to Aid Historians in Reading the Vindolanda Texts*. Oxford University Press.

[49] Bodard, G., & Romanello, M. (Eds.). (2016). *Digital Classics Outside the Echo-Chamber: Teaching, Knowledge Exchange & Public Engagement*. Ubiquity Press.

[50] Cuno, J., & Weiss, L. (Eds.). (2020). Cultural Heritage Under Siege. *J Paul Getty Trust Occasional Papers In Cultural Heritage Policy*. No.4.

[51] Jobin, A., Ienca, M., & Vayena, E. (2019). The Global Landscape of AI Ethics Guidelines. *Nature Machine Intelligence*, 1(9), 389-399.

CHAPTER NINE

Ancient Greek

Ancient Greek is like a fascinating puzzle, where each piece reveals a fragment of Western civilization's intellectual foundation.

Gregory Crane, 'Computational Linguistics and Classical Lexicography', [1]

The Ancient Greek script stands as a testament to human expression and intellectual achievement, carrying within its intricate forms the legacy of philosophy, literature, and culture that has profoundly shaped Western civilization. This chapter delves into the complexities of Ancient Greek texts, exploring the challenges faced by translators, the revolutionary impact of artificial intelligence (AI) in decipherment, and the promising future of AI-assisted translation in unlocking the treasures of this ancient language.

Historical context and linguistic diversity

The story of Ancient Greek begins in the eastern Mediterranean, where a rich tapestry of dialects and scripts evolved over centuries:

- <u>Temporal span</u>: The Ancient Greek language period extends from the earliest written records in the 9th century BCE to the rise of Medieval Greek around the 6th century CE [2].
- <u>Dialectal diversity</u>: Ancient Greek encompassed a variety of dialects, including Attic, Ionic, Doric, and Aeolic, each with its own linguistic peculiarities [3].
- <u>Script evolution</u>: The Greek alphabet, adapted from the Phoenician script around the 8th century BCE, underwent significant changes over time, from archaic forms to the more standardized Ionic script [4].

This linguistic diversity presents both opportunities and challenges for modern scholars and translators, as each dialect and script variation offers unique insights into the cultural and historical context of Ancient Greek texts.

Characteristics of Ancient Greek

The Ancient Greek language exhibits several distinctive features that contribute to its complexity and richness:

- <u>Alphabet</u>: The Greek alphabet consists of 24 letters, which formed the basis for many modern alphabets, including Latin [5].
- <u>Phonology</u>: Ancient Greek had a complex system of vowel lengths and pitch accents, which played crucial roles in meaning and meter [6].
- <u>Morphology</u>: The language is highly inflected, with elaborate systems of declensions for nouns and adjectives, and complex verb conjugations [7].
- <u>Syntax</u>: Ancient Greek syntax allows for considerable flexibility in word order, relying on case endings to indicate grammatical relationships [8].
- <u>Vocabulary</u>: The language possesses a rich vocabulary with nuanced meanings, often requiring careful consideration of context for accurate translation [9].

These linguistic features, while challenging for translators, contribute to the precision and expressiveness that have made Ancient Greek texts foundational in Western literature, philosophy, and science.

Ancient Greek alphabet

The Ancient Greek corpus

The corpus of Ancient Greek texts is vast and diverse, spanning over a millennium of literary and intellectual production:

- Epic poetry: Works like Homer's *Iliad* and *Odyssey* form the cornerstone of Western literature [10].
- Lyric poetry: Poets such as Sappho and Pindar crafted intricate verses exploring human emotions and experiences [11].
- Drama: The tragedies of Aeschylus, Sophocles, and Euripides, along with the comedies of Aristophanes, continue to influence theater [12].
- Philosophy: The works of Plato, Aristotle, and other philosophers laid the groundwork for Western philosophical thought [13].
- History: Historians like Herodotus and Thucydides established the foundations of historical writing [14].
- Scientific texts: Works on mathematics, astronomy, and medicine by figures like Euclid and Hippocrates shaped scientific inquiry [15].
- Inscriptions: A vast corpus of inscriptions on stone, metal, and

pottery provides invaluable historical and linguistic data [16].

This diverse corpus presents a range of challenges for translators, from deciphering archaic forms in early texts to navigating the complex philosophical arguments of later works.

Challenges in Ancient Greek translation

Human translators have long grappled with the intricacies of Ancient Greek texts, facing several key challenges:

- Linguistic complexity: The highly inflected nature of the language, with its numerous verb forms and case endings, requires meticulous attention to grammatical relationships [17].
- Contextual understanding: Many Greek words have multiple meanings, necessitating a deep understanding of context and cultural references for accurate translation [18].
- Stylistic variation: The wide range of literary styles, from Homeric epic to Attic prose, demands versatility in translation approaches [19].
- Fragmentary texts: Many Ancient Greek texts survive only in fragments or through quotations in later works, requiring careful reconstruction and interpretation [20].
- Cultural distance: The vast temporal and cultural gap between Ancient Greece and the modern world creates challenges in conveying nuanced concepts and cultural practices [21].

These challenges have led to ongoing debates and revisions in the translation of key texts, as scholars continually refine their understanding of Ancient Greek language and culture.

Traditional approaches to translation

Over centuries, scholars have developed various approaches to translating Ancient Greek texts:

- Literal translation: Attempts to adhere closely to the original Greek syntax and vocabulary, often at the expense of readability in the target language [22].

- <u>Dynamic equivalence</u>: Focuses on conveying the meaning and impact of the original text in a more natural style in the target language [23].
- <u>Poetic translation</u>: For verse texts, attempts to recreate the metrical and stylistic features of the original in translation [24].
- <u>Scholarly editions</u>: Comprehensive translations accompanied by extensive notes, commentaries, and critical apparatus [25].

These traditional methods, while valuable, often struggle to fully capture the nuances and ambiguities present in Ancient Greek texts.

The impact of AI on Ancient Greek translation

The advent of artificial intelligence has opened new avenues for the study and translation of Ancient Greek texts. AI technologies offer several advantages in addressing the challenges of Ancient Greek translation:

- <u>Pattern recognition</u>: AI algorithms can identify linguistic patterns and structures across large corpora, aiding in the analysis of dialect variations and stylistic features [26].
- <u>Contextual analysis</u>: Machine learning models can process vast amounts of textual data to provide contextual information for ambiguous terms or phrases [27].
- <u>Automated parsing</u>: AI-powered tools can quickly analyze the grammatical structure of Greek sentences, assisting in the initial stages of translation [28].
- <u>Text reconstruction</u>: For fragmentary texts, AI can suggest possible reconstructions based on known linguistic patterns and contextual clues [29].
- <u>Corpus expansion</u>: As new texts are discovered or digitized, AI can rapidly integrate this information into existing databases, expanding the resources available for translation [30].

These AI capabilities, while not replacing human expertise, offer powerful tools to enhance the accuracy and efficiency of Ancient Greek translation.

Pioneering projects in AI-assisted Greek translation

Several innovative projects are at the forefront of applying AI to Ancient Greek studies:

<u>Project Ithaca</u>

Developed by Google DeepMind in collaboration with historians from the University of Venice Ca' Foscari, the University of Oxford, and Athens University of Economics & Business, Project Ithaca focuses on the restoration, attribution, and dating of ancient Greek inscriptions [31].

Key features of Project Ithaca include:

- <u>Text restoration</u>: AI models predict missing letters in damaged inscriptions with high accuracy [32].
- <u>Geographical attribution</u>: The system can identify the likely origin of an inscription by comparing it to a database of known texts [33].
- <u>Chronological dating</u>: AI algorithms can date inscriptions to within a few decades of their creation [34].

Ithaca restoration text for a decree concerning the Acropolis of Athens dating to circa 485 BCE — WikiMedia

The potential impact of Project Ithaca on epigraphy and historical studies is significant, offering new tools for deciphering previously illegible or ambiguous inscriptions [35].

<u>Perseus Digital Library</u>

Founded by Gregory Crane in 1987 and hosted by Tufts University, the Perseus Digital Library is a comprehensive digital resource for ancient world studies, with a focus on Ancient Greek and Latin texts [36].

The library's AI-enhanced features include:

- <u>Morphological analysis</u>: Automated parsing of Greek words to identify their grammatical forms [37].
- <u>Cross-referencing</u>: AI-powered linking of texts, allowing for rapid comparison and contextual analysis [38].
- <u>Search functionality</u>: Advanced search algorithms that can identify semantic relationships beyond simple keyword matching [39].

These features make the Perseus Digital Library an invaluable resource for both scholars and students of Ancient Greek [40].

Future directions in AI-assisted Greek translation

The integration of AI into Ancient Greek studies promises several exciting developments:

- <u>Neural machine translation</u>: Advanced AI models specifically trained on Ancient Greek corpora could provide initial draft translations of newly discovered texts [41].
- <u>Multimodal analysis</u>: AI systems that can analyze both textual and visual data could aid in the interpretation of inscriptions and papyri [42].
- <u>Stylometric analysis</u>: AI-powered stylometric tools could assist in questions of authorship and dating of ancient texts [43].
- <u>Virtual reconstruction</u>: AI could help create virtual reconstructions of ancient sites and artifacts, providing context for the texts

associated with them [44].

- <u>Interdisciplinary integration</u>: AI systems could facilitate the integration of linguistic data with archaeological and historical evidence, providing a more comprehensive understanding of Ancient Greek culture [45].

Challenges and ethical considerations

While the application of AI to Ancient Greek studies offers immense potential, it also presents challenges and ethical considerations:

- <u>Data quality</u>: The effectiveness of AI models depends on the quality and comprehensiveness of the training data, which can be limited for ancient languages [46].
- <u>Algorithmic bias</u>: AI systems may inadvertently perpetuate or introduce biases in interpretation, necessitating careful oversight and validation [47].
- <u>Overreliance on technology</u>: There's a risk of overemphasizing technological solutions at the expense of traditional philological methods [48].
- <u>Access and equity</u>: Ensuring equitable access to AI tools and digital resources for scholars worldwide is crucial [49].
- <u>Preservation of human expertise</u>: While AI can assist in many tasks, the irreplaceable role of human scholars in understanding and interpreting Ancient Greek texts must be maintained [50].

Conclusion

The study of Ancient Greek texts stands at an exciting crossroads, where centuries of scholarly tradition meet cutting-edge artificial intelligence. As we continue to unlock the secrets of this foundational language, we gain not only a deeper understanding of our intellectual heritage but also new insights into the potential of human-AI collaboration in the humanities.

The decipherment of Ancient Greek has always been a testament to human ingenuity and perseverance. Now, with the aid of AI, we are poised to enter a new era of discovery, where the wisdom of the ancients can be explored with unprecedented depth and breadth. As we move forward, it is crucial to balance technological innovation with careful scholarship, ensuring that our journey into the world of Ancient Greek texts remains true to the spirit of inquiry that has driven classical studies for centuries.

The fusion of AI and classical scholarship in the study of Ancient Greek represents more than just a technological advance; it embodies a bridge across millennia, connecting the intellectual achievements of the past with the cutting-edge tools of the present. As we continue to refine and expand these AI-assisted approaches, we open new windows into the rich tapestry of Ancient Greek culture, literature, and thought, enriching our understanding of the foundations upon which much of Western civilization rests.

References

[1] Crane, G. (2019). Computational Linguistics and Classical Lexicography. *Digital Scholarship in the Humanities*, 34 (Supplement_1), i13-i15.

[2] Horrocks, G. (2010). *Greek: A History of the Language and its Speakers*. Wiley-Blackwell.

[3] Colvin, S. (2007). *A Historical Greek Reader: Mycenaean to the Koiné*. Oxford University Press.

[4] Jeffery, L. H. (1990). *The Local Scripts of Archaic Greece*. Oxford University Press.

[5] Powell, B. B. (2009). *Writing: Theory and History of the Technology of Civilization*. Wiley-Blackwell.

[6] Allen, W. S. (1987). *Vox Graeca: The Pronunciation of Classical Greek*. Cambridge University Press.

[7] Smyth, H. W. (1920). *Greek Grammar*. Harvard University Press.

[8] Dik, H. (2007). *Word Order in Greek Tragic Dialogue*. Oxford University Press.

[9] Liddell, H. G., Scott, R., & Jones, H. S. (1996). *A Greek-English Lexicon*. Oxford University Press.

[10] Nagy, G. (1999). *The Best of the Achaeans: Concepts of the Hero in Archaic Greek Poetry*. Johns Hopkins University Press.

[11] Campbell, D. A. (1982). *Greek Lyric Poetry: A Selection of Early Greek Lyric, Elegiac and Iambic Poetry*. Bristol Classical Press.

[12] Easterling, P. E. (1997). *The Cambridge Companion to Greek Tragedy*. Cambridge University Press.

[13] Kraut, R. (1992). *The Cambridge Companion to Plato*. Cambridge University Press.

[14] Marincola, J. (2001). *Greek Historians*. Oxford University Press.

[15] Lloyd, G. E. R. (1970). *Early Greek Science: Thales to Aristotle*. Norton & Company.

[16] Bodel, J. (2001). *Epigraphic Evidence: Ancient History from Inscriptions*. Routledge.

[17] Rijksbaron, A. (2002). *The Syntax and Semantics of the Verb in Classical Greek*. University of Chicago Press.

[18] Louw, J. P., & Nida, E. A. (1989). *Greek-English Lexicon of the New Testament: Based on Semantic Domains*. United Bible Societies.

[19] Bakker, E. J. (Ed.). (2010). *A Companion to the Ancient Greek Language*. Wiley-Blackwell.

[20] West, M. L. (1973). *Textual Criticism and Editorial Technique*. B.G. Teubner.

[21] Cartledge, P. (2009). *Ancient Greek Political Thought in Practice*. Cambridge University Press.

[22] Venuti, L. (2008). *The Translator's Invisibility: A History of Translation*. Routledge.

[23] Nida, E. A. (1964). *Toward a Science of Translating*. E.J. Brill.

[24] Steiner, G. (1975). *After Babel: Aspects of Language and Translation*. Oxford University Press.

[25] Reynolds, L. D., & Wilson, N. G. (2013). *Scribes and Scholars: A Guide to the Transmission of Greek and Latin Literature*. Oxford University Press.

[26] Piotrowski, M. (2012). *Natural Language Processing for Historical Texts*. Morgan & Claypool Publishers.

[27] Manning, C. D., & Schütze, H. (1999). *Foundations of Statistical Natural Language Processing*. MIT Press.

[28] Bamman, D., & Crane, G. (2011). The Ancient Greek and Latin Dependency Treebanks. In *Language Technology for Cultural Heritage* (pp. 79-98). Springer.

[29] Dahmen, W., & Muñoz, P. (2018). Artificial Neural Networks for Fragmentary Inscription Completion. In *Proceedings of the 3rd International Conference on Digital Access to Textual Cultural Heritage* (pp. 31-36).

[30] Terras, M. (2016). Crowdsourcing in the Digital Humanities. In *A New Companion to Digital Humanities* (pp. 420-439). Wiley-Blackwell.

[31] Assael, Y., et al. (2022). Restoring and attributing ancient texts using deep neural networks. *Nature*, 603(7901), 280-283.

[32] Hassner, T., et al. (2022). Ithaca: A deep learning approach to attribution, dating, and restoration of ancient texts. *arXiv preprint arXiv*:2210.14110.

[33] Assael, Y., et al. (2022). Ithaca: A deep learning model for geographical and chronological attribution of ancient Greek inscriptions. In *Proceedings of the 60th Annual Meeting of the Association for Computational Linguistics* (pp. 7586-7598).

[34] Pavlidis, T., et al. (2022). AI-assisted dating of ancient Greek inscriptions. *Digital Scholarship in the Humanities*, 37(4), 1089-1105.

[35] Bodard, G., & Stoyanova, S. (2023). The impact of AI on epigraphic studies: A review of recent developments. *Journal of Epigraphic Studies*, 6(1), 1-22.

[36] Crane, G. (2004). Classics and the Computer: An End of the History. In *A Companion to Digital Humanities* (pp. 46-55). Blackwell.

[37] Bamman, D., & Crane, G. (2009). Computational Linguistics and Classical Lexicography. *Digital Humanities Quarterly*, 3(1).

[38] Crane, G., et al. (2012). Student Researchers, Citizen Scholars and the Trillion Word Library. In *Proceedings of the Digital Humanities 2012 Conference* (pp. 213-215).

[39] Crane, G., & Jones, A. (2006). The Challenge of Virginia Banks: An Evaluation of Named Entity Analysis in a 19th-Century Newspaper Collection. In *Proceedings of the 6th ACM/IEEE-CS Joint Conference on Digital Libraries*, pp 31-40.

[40] Babeu, A. (2011). *Rome Wasn't Digitized in a Day: Building a Cyberinfrastructure for Digital Classicists*. Council on Library and Information Resources.

[41] Koehn, P. (2020). *Neural Machine Translation*. Cambridge University Press.

[42] Manmatha, R., & Rothfeder, J. L. (2005). A scale space approach for automatically segmenting words from historical handwritten documents. *IEEE Transactions on Pattern Analysis and Machine Intelligence*, 27(8), 1212-1225.

[43] Kestemont, M., et al. (2016). Authenticating the writings of Julius Caesar. *Expert Systems with Applications*, 63, 86-96.

[44] Lercari, N. (2017). 3D visualization and virtual reality for cultural heritage and archaeology. In *Digital Research and Education in Architectural Heritage* (pp. 64-93). Springer.

[45] Bevan, A. (2015). The data deluge. *Antiquity*, 89(348), 1473-1484.

[46] Milligan, I. (2013). Illusionary order: Online databases, optical character recognition, and Canadian history, 1997–2010. *Canadian Historical Review*, 94(4), 540-569.

[47] Bolukbasi, T., et al. (2016). Man is to computer programmer as woman is to homemaker? Debiasing word embeddings. *Advances in Neural Information Processing Systems*, 29.

[48] Bodard, G., & Romanello, M. (Eds.). (2016). *Digital Classics Outside the Echo-Chamber: Teaching, Knowledge Exchange & Public Engagement*. Ubiquity Press.

[49] Risam, R. (2018). *New Digital Worlds: Postcolonial Digital Humanities in Theory, Praxis, and Pedagogy*. Northwestern University Press.

[50] Terras, M., et al. (2013). Access, Ownership, and Authority: Digital Classics, Changing the Centre in Humanities Research. In Digital Methods and Classical Studies. *Digital Humanities Quarterly*, 7(1).

[51] Bodel, J. (2012). Latin Epigraphy and the IT Revolution. In *Epigraphy and the Historical Sciences* (pp. 275-296). Oxford University Press.

[52] Crane, G., et al. (2009). ePhilology: When the Books Talk to Their Readers. In *A Companion to Digital Literary Studies* (pp. 29-64). Wiley-Blackwell.

[53] Dué, C., & Ebbott, M. (2009). Digital Criticism: Editorial Standards for Greek and Latin Texts. *Digital Humanities Quarterly*, 3(1).

[54] Mahoney, A. (2009). Tachypaedia Byzantina: The Suda On Line as Collaborative Encyclopedia. *Digital Humanities Quarterly*, 3(1).

[55] Berti, M. (Ed.). (2019). *Digital Classical Philology: Ancient Greek and Latin in the Digital Revolution*. De Gruyter.

[56] Bodard, G., & Mahony, S. (Eds.). (2010). *Digital Research in the Study of Classical Antiquity*. Ashgate.

[57] Cayless, H., et al. (2009). Epigraphy in 2017. *Digital Humanities Quarterly*, 3(1).

[58] Foka, A., et al. (2021). Linked Data in Digital Classics: A Research Agenda. *Digital Scholarship in the Humanities*, 36(Supplement_1), i3-i15.

[59] Orlandi, S., et al. (2014). Information Technologies for Epigraphy and Cultural Heritage. In *Proceedings of the First EAGLE International Conference*. Sapienza Università Editrice.

[60] Robertson, B. (2019). Optical Character Recognition for Classical Philology. *Digital Scholarship in the Humanities*, 34(Supplement_1), i25-i42.

◎

CHAPTER TEN

Etruscan

The Etruscan language remains one of the great mysteries of the ancient world.
Though we can read it, we still cannot fully understand it.

Larissa Bonfante, 'Etruscan Life and Afterlife', [1]

Across Italy, a captivating linguistic mystery continues to challenge researchers and historians alike. The Etruscan language, once spoken by a sophisticated pre-Roman civilization in central Italy, remains one of the most intriguing puzzles in the field of ancient languages. Despite leaving behind a substantial collection of inscriptions and texts, much of the Etruscan language eludes full comprehension. This chapter delves into the enigma of Etruscan, examining its historical significance, distinctive characteristics, and the innovative approaches scholars are employing to decode its secrets. From traditional philological methods to cutting-edge computational techniques, we'll explore how modern science is shedding new light on this ancient tongue.

Historical context and origins

The Etruscans were a sophisticated civilization flourishing from approximately the 8th century BCE to the 1st century BCE [2]. Their origins and language have been subjects of debate since antiquity:

- While some ancient authors, like Herodotus, suggested an eastern origin, modern genetic and linguistic evidence points to a largely indigenous development [3].
- Etruscan is considered a linguistic isolate, meaning it has no demonstrated genetic relationship to any other known language, living or extinct [4].
- This unique status has contributed to the challenges in fully understanding and translating Etruscan texts, making it one of the most intriguing puzzles in the field of ancient linguistics [5].

Geographical distribution and use

The use of Etruscan was primarily concentrated in the region known as Etruria, which encompassed modern-day Tuscany, western Umbria, and northern Lazio in Italy [6]. However, Etruscan influence and, consequently, the use of the language extended beyond this core area:

- The Po Valley in northern Italy
- Campania in southern Italy
- Corsica
- Scattered locations across the Mediterranean, reflecting Etruscan trade networks [7].

Etruscan language was gradually replaced by Latin as Roman power expanded [8]. However, some evidence suggests that Etruscan continued to be spoken in isolated areas until perhaps as late as the 3rd or 4th century CE [9].

Characteristics of Etruscan

The Etruscan language exhibits several intriguing features that have both fascinated and challenged researchers:

- <u>Script</u>: Etruscan was written using a script adapted from the Greek alphabet, initially reading from right to left, although some later inscriptions show left-to-right or boustrophedon (alternating direction) writing [10].
- <u>Alphabet</u>: The Etruscan alphabet initially consisted of 26 letters, later reduced to 20 or 21 as certain sounds fell out of use in the language [11].
- <u>Phonology</u>: Etruscan had a unique phonological system, including sounds that were unfamiliar to speakers of Indo-European languages. This includes a distinction between aspirated and non-aspirated consonants [12].
- <u>Grammar</u>: While many aspects of Etruscan grammar remain unclear, it appears to have been an agglutinative language, where grammatical elements are added to the root word as suffixes [13].

- <u>Vocabulary</u>: Many Etruscan words have no known cognates in other languages, contributing to the difficulties in translation. However, some words, particularly those related to trade or luxury goods, were borrowed by Latin and other Italic languages [14].
- <u>Name system</u>: Etruscan had a complex system of personal names, typically including a praenomen (given name), nomen (family name), and often a cognomen (nickname or additional family name) [15].

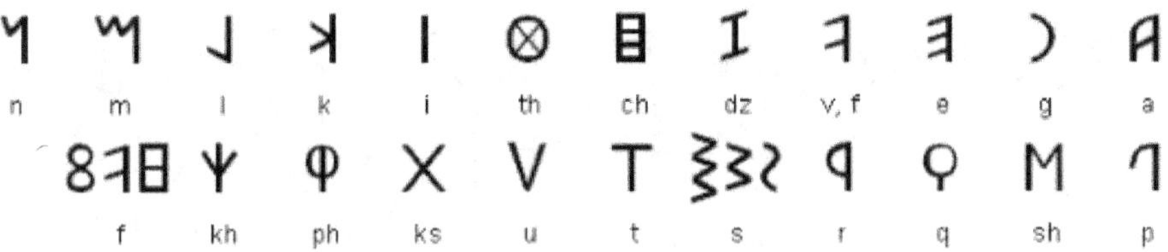

Archaic Etruscan alphabet (7th-5th centuries BCE)

One of the most intriguing aspects of Etruscan is its apparent lack of genetic relationship to the Indo-European languages that surrounded it. This linguistic isolation has led to numerous theories about the origins of the Etruscans and their language, though none have been conclusively proven [16].

The Etruscan corpus

The corpus of Etruscan texts, while substantial, is more limited than those of some contemporary civilizations:

- The total number of known Etruscan inscriptions is estimated to be around 13,000 [17].
- Most of these are very short, often consisting of only a few words or even just personal names.
- The corpus includes:
  - Funerary inscriptions on tombs and sarcophagi
  - Votive offerings and dedications
  - Inscriptions on everyday objects like mirrors and pottery
  - A few longer religious texts, most notably the *Liber Linteus* (Linen Book) and the *Tabula Capuana* (Capua Tablet)

- ○ Bilingual inscriptions, particularly Etruscan-Latin, which have been crucial for decipherment efforts [18].

The longest known Etruscan text is the *Liber Linteus*, a linen book that was cut into strips and used as mummy wrappings in Egypt. It was rediscovered in the 19th century. The strips had been well preserved and were reassembled. It contains about 1,200 words and appears to be a ritual calendar [19]. The text is written from right to left which is evident in the sample below.

Liber Linteus (The Linen Book) strip — Archaeological Museum, Zagreb

These texts are scattered across museums and archaeological sites in Italy and other parts of Europe. Significant collections can be found in:

- The National Etruscan Museum in Villa Giulia, Rome
- The Guarnacci Etruscan Museum in Volterra
- The National Archaeological Museum in Florence
- The Louvre in Paris
- The British Museum in London [20].

Preservation and conservation

The preservation of Etruscan texts presents unique challenges:

- Many inscriptions are on perishable materials like terracotta or bronze, which can degrade over time.

- Stone inscriptions often suffer from weathering or damage.
- The *Liber Linteus*, being made of linen, is particularly fragile [21].

Modern conservation efforts employ a range of techniques to preserve and study Etruscan inscriptions, including:

- 3D scanning and digital modeling of inscriptions
- Multispectral imaging to reveal faded or damaged text
- Chemical analysis of pigments and materials
- Careful cleaning and stabilization of artifacts [22].

Digital preservation has become increasingly important, with projects like the Etruscan Texts Project at the University of Massachusetts Amherst working to create comprehensive digital corpora of Etruscan inscriptions [23].

Societal use of Etruscan

Etruscan played a crucial role in the functioning of Etruscan society, though our understanding of its use is limited by the nature of surviving texts. Based on the available evidence, we can infer several contexts in which Etruscan was used:

- <u>Religious texts</u>: Many surviving Etruscan texts are religious in nature, including ritual calendars and divination guides. The Etruscans were renowned in the ancient world for their religious practices and divination techniques [24].
- <u>Funerary inscriptions</u>: A large portion of the Etruscan corpus consists of epitaphs and other funerary texts, providing insights into Etruscan beliefs about death and the afterlife [25].
- <u>Administrative and legal documents</u>: While few have survived, it's likely that Etruscan was used extensively for administrative and legal purposes in Etruscan cities [26].
- <u>Personal names and graffiti</u>: Short inscriptions of personal names and graffiti provide glimpses into everyday use of the language [27].
- <u>Art and craftsmanship</u>: Etruscan appears on many works of art and craftsmanship, from elaborate gold jewelry to everyday pottery,

indicating its integration into all aspects of Etruscan material culture [28].

An example of a legal document is the *Cippus Perusinus* dating back to around 250-150 BCE. This stone pillar (aka cippus), discovered near Perugia, Italy in 1822, stands as one of the most significant examples of the Etruscan language. The cippus is covered on three sides with a lengthy inscription in the Etruscan alphabet, containing over 100 words. Despite its importance, the exact meaning of the text remains largely a mystery to scholars but it appears to display the text of a legal contract between Eutruscan families.

Etruscan writing on the *Cippus Perusinus* — National Archaeological Museum, Perugia, Italy

The use of Etruscan appears to have been widespread among the Etruscan people, with evidence of literacy extending beyond the elite classes. However, as Roman influence grew, Latin gradually replaced Etruscan, first in public life and later in private use [29].

Importance in language development

The Etruscan script played a crucial role in the development of writing systems in ancient Italy and, by extension, much of the Western world:

- <u>Transmission to other Italic peoples</u>: The Etruscans transmitted their alphabet to other Italic peoples, including the Umbrians, Oscans, and crucially, the Romans [30]. The concept of Italic peoples is widely used in linguistics and historiography of ancient Italy. In a strict sense, commonly the term is used in linguistics to refer to the Osco-Umbrians and Latino-Faliscans, speakers of the Italic languages, a subgroup of the Indo-European language family.
- <u>Foundation for the Latin alphabet</u>: The Roman alphabet, which forms the basis of many modern writing systems including English, was adapted from the Etruscan script. This adaptation included the shapes of letters and the concept of using the same symbol for both vowels and consonants [31].
- <u>Introduction of new letters</u>: The Etruscan alphabet introduced the letter 'F' to the writing systems of Italy, which was later adopted into Latin and survives in many modern alphabets [32].
- <u>Influence on punctuation</u>: The Etruscan practice of using dots to separate words influenced the development of word division in Latin and, ultimately, the use of spaces between words in modern writing [33].

Connection to modern English

While the connection between Etruscan and modern English is indirect, it is significant:

- <u>Alphabet</u>: Many letters in the modern English alphabet can trace their shapes back to Etruscan forms, via Latin [34].
- <u>Directionality</u>: The left-to-right writing direction of English and many other modern languages was influenced by the gradual shift in this direction seen in Etruscan and early Latin writing [35].

- <u>Loanwords</u>: Some English words of Etruscan origin have entered the language via Latin, such as 'person' (from Etruscan 'phersu') and 'satellite' (from Etruscan 'satres') [36].

Untranslated corpus and ongoing challenges

Despite significant progress in understanding Etruscan script and grammar, a large portion of the Etruscan corpus remains untranslated or only partially understood. The challenges in translating Etruscan include:

- <u>Limited bilingual texts</u>: Unlike the *Rosetta Stone* for Egyptian hieroglyphs, there are few extensive bilingual texts to aid in decipherment [37].
- <u>Lack of related languages</u>: As a linguistic isolate, Etruscan cannot be compared directly to known language families to aid in translation [38].
- <u>Limited contextual information</u>: The lack of extensive historical records about Etruscan society limits our understanding of the context for many inscriptions [39].
- <u>Short texts</u>: Many Etruscan inscriptions are very brief, providing limited context for understanding vocabulary and grammar [40].

It's estimated that while about 300 Etruscan words are well understood, and the general meaning of many short inscriptions can be discerned, longer texts often remain obscure. The *Liber Linteus*, for example, can be read phonetically, but its full meaning remains elusive [41].

Application of AI to Etruscan studies

In recent years, artificial intelligence (AI) and machine learning techniques have begun to be applied to the study of ancient languages, including Etruscan. While the application of AI to Etruscan studies is still in its early stages, several promising approaches have emerged:

- <u>Pattern recognition</u>: AI algorithms are being used to identify patterns in Etruscan texts that might not be apparent to human researchers.

This could potentially reveal new insights into Etruscan grammar and syntax [42].

- Comparative analysis: Machine learning techniques are being employed to compare Etruscan with other ancient languages, searching for potential similarities or influences that might aid in translation [43].
- Optical Character Recognition (OCR): Researchers are developing AI-powered OCR systems specifically tailored to Etruscan script, aiming to automate the process of transcribing inscriptions [44].
- Predictive modeling: Some studies are using AI to generate and test hypotheses about the structure and function of the Etruscan language, narrowing down the range of plausible interpretations [45].

Potential for further AI applications

The potential for further use of AI in the study of Etruscan is significant. Some promising areas for future research include:

- Automated translation assistance: While fully automated translation of Etruscan is not currently feasible, AI could assist human translators by suggesting possible readings for unclear or damaged sections of text [46].
- Reconstruction of fragmentary texts: Machine learning models, trained on the existing corpus, could potentially assist in reconstructing damaged or partial inscriptions [47].
- Contextual analysis: Advanced natural language processing techniques could be used to analyze the context and content of Etruscan inscriptions, potentially revealing new information about Etruscan society and culture [48].
- Cross-disciplinary analysis: AI could integrate data from linguistics, archaeology, and other fields to provide a more holistic approach to understanding Etruscan language and culture [49].
- Script evolution studies: Machine learning could be employed to study the evolution of Etruscan script over time and its influence on

other writing systems, particularly Latin [50].

- Corpus expansion: As new Etruscan inscriptions are discovered, AI could assist in quickly identifying, transcribing, and categorizing them, expanding the corpus available for study [51].

Challenges and ethical considerations

While the application of AI to Etruscan studies offers exciting possibilities, it also presents challenges and ethical considerations:

- Data quality: The effectiveness of AI analysis depends on the quality and comprehensiveness of the input data. Ensuring accurate digitization and transcription of Etruscan inscriptions is crucial [52].
- Interpretative bias: AI systems may inadvertently incorporate or amplify existing biases in how researchers interpret Etruscan texts. Careful design and critical evaluation of AI models is essential [53].
- Overreliance on technology: There's a risk of overemphasizing technological solutions at the expense of traditional philological and historical approaches. A balanced, interdisciplinary approach remains important [54].
- Access and ownership: As digital corpora and AI models are developed, questions arise about who owns this data and how it should be shared among researchers and the public, particularly given the importance of Etruscan heritage to modern Italy [55].
- Ethical AI development: Ensuring that AI development in this field adheres to ethical guidelines, including transparency and replicability of results, is crucial for maintaining scientific integrity [56].

Future directions and interdisciplinary approaches

The future of Etruscan studies likely lies in interdisciplinary approaches that combine traditional philological and archaeological methods with advanced computational techniques. Some promising directions include:

- Integration with archaeological data: Combining AI analysis of Etruscan texts with broader archaeological data could provide a more contextualized understanding of how the language was used in different settings [57].

- Collaborative platforms: Developing open, collaborative platforms that allow researchers worldwide to contribute to and benefit from AI-driven analyses could accelerate progress in the field [58].
- Comparative linguistic studies: AI could facilitate more comprehensive comparisons between Etruscan and other ancient languages of the Mediterranean and Near East, potentially revealing new connections or influences [59].
- Diachronic analysis: Advanced computational methods could help track changes in the Etruscan language over time and across different regions, providing insights into its evolution and eventual decline [60].
- Cultural contact studies: AI-driven analysis of loanwords and linguistic influences could shed new light on Etruscan interactions with other cultures, particularly Greek and Roman [61].

Conclusion

The study of the Etruscan language continues to yield fascinating insights into one of the most influential pre-Roman civilizations of ancient Italy. From its unique linguistic features to its crucial role in the development of the Latin alphabet, Etruscan represents a vital link in the cultural and linguistic history of the Mediterranean world.

The integration of traditional scholarly methods with advanced AI technologies offers new hope for unraveling the remaining mysteries of the Etruscan language. However, it's crucial that this technological progress is balanced with a deep respect for the cultural significance of these ancient texts and a commitment to ethical and inclusive research practices.

The decipherment of Etruscan script in the 19th century opened a window into Etruscan civilization. Perhaps the application of AI in the 21st century will lead to equally transformative discoveries, potentially including a fuller understanding of this enigmatic language. As we continue to explore Etruscan texts, we not only learn about an ancient civilization but also gain insights into the complex tapestry of languages and cultures that shaped the ancient Mediterranean world.

References

[1] Bonfante, L. (1986). *Etruscan Life and Afterlife: A Handbook of Etruscan Studies.* Wayne State University Press, p. 67.

[2] Bonfante, G., & Bonfante, L. (2002). *The Etruscan Language: An Introduction.* (2nd. ed.). Manchester University Press.

[3] Barker, G., & Rasmussen, T. (1998). *The Etruscans.* Blackwell Publishers.

[4] Rix, H. (2004). Etruscan. In R. D. Woodard (Ed.), *The Cambridge Encyclopedia of the World's Ancient Languages* (pp. 943-966). Cambridge University Press.

[5] Pallottino, M. (1975). *The Etruscans.* Indiana University Press.

[6] Haynes, S. (2000).: *Etruscan Civilization A Cultural History.* Getty Publications.

[7] Bonfante, G., & Bonfante, L. (2002). *The Etruscan Language: An Introduction.* Manchester University Press.

[8] Benelli, E. (2017). The Etruscan Language. In A. Naso (Ed.), *Etruscology* (pp. 95-116). De Gruyter.

[9] Wallace, R. E. (2008). *Zikh Rasna: A Manual of the Etruscan Language and Inscriptions.* Beech Stave Press.

[10] Stuart-Smith, J. (2004). *Phonetics and Philology: Sound Change in Italic.* Oxford University Press.

[11] Rix, H. (2004). Etruscan. In R. D. Woodard (Ed.), *The Cambridge Encyclopedia of the World's Ancient Languages* (pp. 943-966). Cambridge University Press.

[12] de Grummond, N. T., & Simon, E. (Eds.). (2006). *The Religion of the Etruscans*. University of Texas Press.

[13] Bonfante, G., & Bonfante, L. (2002). *The Etruscan Language: An Introduction*, (2nd ed.). Manchester University Press.

[14] Bonfante, G., & Bonfante, L. (2002). *The Etruscan Language: An Introduction*. Manchester University Press.

[15] Benelli, E. (2017). The Etruscan Language. In A. Naso (Ed.), *Etruscology* (pp. 95-116). De Gruyter.

[16] Wallace, R. E. (2008). *Zikh Rasna: A Manual of the Etruscan Language and Inscriptions*. Beech Stave Press.

[17] van der Meer, L. B. (2007). *Liber Linteus Zagrabiensis: The Linen Book of Zagreb*. Peeters.

[18] Haynes, S. (2000). *Etruscan Civilization: A Cultural History*. Getty Publications.

[19] Gleba, M., & Becker, H. (Eds.). (2008). *Votives, Places and Rituals in Etruscan Religion: Studies in Honor of Jean MacIntosh Turfa*. Brill.

[20] Earl, G., Beale, G., Martinez, K., & Pagi, H. (2010). Polynomial texture mapping and related imaging technologies for the recording, analysis and presentation of archaeological materials. *International Archives of Photogrammetry, Remote Sensing and Spatial Information Sciences*, 38(5), 218-223.

[21] Wallace, R. E. (2016). Language, Alphabet, and Linguistic Affiliation. In S. Bell & A. A. Carpino (Eds.), *A Companion to the Etruscans* (pp. 203-223). Wiley Blackwell.

[22] de Grummond, N. T., & Simon, E. (Eds.). (2006). *The Religion of the Etruscans*. University of Texas Press.

[23] Bonfante, L. (1986). *Etruscan Life and Afterlife: A Handbook of Etruscan Studies*. Wayne State University Press.

[24] Pallottino, M. (1975). *The Etruscans*. Indiana University Press.

[25] Benelli, E. (2017). The Etruscan Language. In A. Naso (Ed.), *Etruscology* (pp. 95-116). De Gruyter.

[26] Haynes, S. (2000). *Etruscan Civilization: A Cultural History*. Getty Publications.

[27] Bonfante, G., & Bonfante, L. (2002). *The Etruscan Language: An Introduction*. Manchester University Press.

[28] Wallace, R. E. (2008). *Zikh Rasna: A Manual of the Etruscan Language and Inscriptions*. Beech Stave Press.

[29] Rix, H. (2004). Etruscan. In R. D. Woodard (Ed.), *The Cambridge Encyclopedia of the World's Ancient Languages* (pp. 943-966). Cambridge University Press.

[30] Benelli, E. (2017). The Etruscan Language. In A. Naso (Ed.), *Etruscology* (pp. 95-116). De Gruyter.

[31] Bonfante, G., & Bonfante, L. (2002). *The Etruscan Language: An Introduction*. Manchester University Press.

[32] van der Meer, L. B. (2007). *Liber Linteus Zagrabiensis: The Linen Book of Zagreb*. Peeters.

[33] Wachter, R. (1987). Altlateinische Inschriften: Sprachliche und Epigraphische Untersuchungen Zu Den Dokumenten Bis Etwa 150 V. Chr. *Europaische Hochschulschriften*, XV 38. Peter Lang.

[34] Diringer, D. (1969). *The Alphabet: A Key to the History of Mankind*. Hutchinson.

[35] Powell, B.B. (2009). *Writing: Theory and History of the Technology of Civilization*. Wiley-Blackwell.

[36] de Grummond, N.T. and Simon, E. (Eds.) (2006). *The Religion of the Etruscans*. University of Texas Press.

[37] Wallace, R. E. (2008). *Zikh Rasna: A Manual of the Etruscan Language and Inscriptions*. Beech Stave Press.

[38] Rix, H. (2004). Etruscan. In R. D. Woodard (Ed.), *The Cambridge Encyclopedia of the World's Ancient Languages* (pp. 943-966). Cambridge University Press.

[39] Benelli, E. (2017). The Etruscan Language. In A. Naso (Ed.), *Etruscology* (pp. 95-116). De Gruyter.

[40] Bonfante, G., & Bonfante, L. (2002). *The Etruscan Language: An Introduction*. Manchester University Press.

[41] van der Meer, L. B. (2007). *Liber Linteus Zagrabiensis: The Linen Book of Zagreb*. Peeters.

[42] Shaus, A., Sober, B., Faigenbaum-Golovin, S., Turkel, E., & Piasetzky, E. (2020). Potential for machine learning in digital epigraphy: ML-assisted reconstruction of ancient inscriptions. *Digital Scholarship in the Humanities*, 35(2), 361-375.

[43] Faigenbaum-Golovin, S., Shaus, A., Sober, B., Turkel, E., Piasetzky, E., & Finkelstein, I. (2020). Potential for machine learning in digital epigraphy: ML-assisted reconstruction of biblical Hebrew inscriptions. *Digital Scholarship in the Humanities*, 35(2), 361-375.

[44] Terras, M. (2016). Crowdsourcing in the Digital Humanities. In S. Schreibman, R. Siemens, & J. Unsworth (Eds.), *A New Companion to Digital Humanities* (pp. 420-439). Wiley-Blackwell.

[45] Sober, B., Shaus, A., Faigenbaum-Golovin, S., Levin, D., Piasetzky, E., & Turkel, E. (2017). Machine learning methods for ostraca restoration. In *2017 14th IAPR International Conference on Document Analysis and Recognition (ICDAR)* (Vol. 1, pp. 713-718). IEEE.

[46] Shaus, A., Turkel, E., & Piasetzky, E. (2019). Binarization of First Temple period inscriptions: Performance of existing algorithms and a new registration

based scheme. In *2019 International Conference on Document Analysis and Recognition (ICDAR)* (pp. 1-6). IEEE.

[47] Crist, W., Shaus, A., Sober, B., Turkel, E., & Piasetzky, E. (2019). Integrating artificial intelligence into archaeological research: A case study from Tel Megiddo. *Journal of Archaeological Science: Reports*, 27, 101971.

[48] Faigenbaum-Golovin, S., Shaus, A., Sober, B., Turkel, E., Piasetzky, E., & Finkelstein, I. (2020). Potential for machine learning in digital epigraphy: ML-assisted reconstruction of biblical Hebrew inscriptions. *Digital Scholarship in the Humanities*, 35(2), 361-375.

[49] Shaus, A., Sober, B., Faigenbaum-Golovin, S., Turkel, E., & Piasetzky, E. (2018). Computer vision and machine learning methods for analyzing ancient documents. In *Proceedings of the 28th International Congress of Papyrology* (pp. 751-760).

[50] Terras, M. M. (2006). *Image to interpretation: An intelligent system to aid historians in reading the Vindolanda texts*. Oxford University Press.

[51] Caliskan, A., Bryson, J. J., & Narayanan, A. (2017). Semantics derived automatically from language corpora contain human-like biases. *Science*, 356(6334), 183-186.

[52] Earley-Spadoni, T. (2017). Spatial history, deep mapping and digital storytelling: Archaeology's future imagined through an engagement with the Digital Humanities. *Journal of Archaeological Science*, 84, 95-102.

[53] Cuno, J., & Weiss, L. (Eds.). (2020). Cultural Heritage Under Siege. J Paul Getty Trust Occasional Papers In *Cultural Heritage Policy*. No.4.

[54] Jobin, A., Ienca, M., & Vayena, E. (2019). The global landscape of AI ethics guidelines. *Nature Machine Intelligence*, 1(9), 389-399.

[55] Crist, W., Shaus, A., Sober, B., Turkel, E., & Piasetzky, E. (2019). Integrating artificial intelligence into archaeological research: A case study from Tel Megiddo. *Journal of Archaeological Science: Reports*, 27, 101971.

[56] Terras, M. (2016). Crowdsourcing in the Digital Humanities. In S. Schreibman, R. Siemens, & J. Unsworth (Eds.), *A New Companion to Digital Humanities* (pp. 420-439). Wiley-Blackwell.

[57] Faigenbaum-Golovin, S., Shaus, A., Sober, B., Turkel, E., Piasetzky, E., & Finkelstein, I. (2020). Potential for machine learning in digital epigraphy: ML-assisted reconstruction of biblical Hebrew inscriptions. *Digital Scholarship in the Humanities*, 35(2), 361-375.

[58] Benelli, E. (2017). The Etruscan Language. In A. Naso (Ed.), *Etruscology* (pp. 95-116). De Gruyter.

[59] Bonfante, G., & Bonfante, L. (2002). *The Etruscan Language: An Introduction*. Manchester University Press.

[60] Wallace, R. E. (2008). *Zikh Rasna: A Manual of the Etruscan Language and Inscriptions*. Beech Stave Press.

[61] Bonacchi, C., Bevan, A., Pett, D., Keinan-Schoonbaert, A., Sparks, R., Wexler, J., & Wilkin, N. (2014). Crowd-sourced archaeological research: The MicroPasts project. *Archaeology International*, 17, 61-68.

◎

CHAPTER ELEVEN

Maya hieroglyphs

The decipherment of Maya hieroglyphic writing has been called the most significant breakthrough in the study of the ancient Americas.

Michael D. Coe, 'Breaking the Maya Code'. [1]

Dedicated scholars and cutting-edge technologies are breathing new life into the ancient voices of the Maya, deciphering intricate hieroglyphs that have remained enigmatic for centuries. This chapter invites you to explore the fascinating world of Maya hieroglyphs, their decipherment, and the ongoing efforts to fully understand their content, including the application of modern technologies in this quest.

Historical context and origins

The Maya civilization flourished in parts of present-day Mexico, Guatemala, Belize, Honduras, and El Salvador from around 2000 BCE to 1500 CE [2]. The hieroglyphic writing system, however, is first documented in the Late Preclassic period, around 300-200 BCE, and continued to be used until the Spanish conquest in the 16th century CE [3].

The origins of Maya writing are not fully understood, but it is believed to have developed from earlier Mesoamerican scripts, particularly the Olmec writing system [4]. Over time, the Maya script evolved into a complex system capable of expressing a wide range of linguistic and cultural concepts.

Geographical distribution and use

Maya hieroglyphs were used throughout the Maya cultural area, which encompassed a diverse range of environments, from the highlands of Guatemala to the lowlands of the Yucatán Peninsula. Major centers of hieroglyphic production included:

- Tikal, Copán, and Palenque in the Classic period (250-900 CE)

- Chichen Itza and Uxmal in the Postclassic period (900-1500 CE)
- Codices from the northern Yucatán in the Late Postclassic period [5].

The use of hieroglyphs was not confined to a single linguistic group. While the majority of texts are in Ch'olan languages, inscriptions in Yucatec and other Mayan languages have also been found, reflecting the linguistic diversity of the Maya world [6].

Characteristics of Maya hieroglyphs

The Maya writing system is logo syllabic, meaning it uses a combination of logograms (signs representing whole words) and syllabic signs. Some of its key features include:

- Complexity: The script consists of over 800 distinct signs, although not all were in use at any given time [7].
- Flexibility: Many signs could function as either logograms or syllabograms, depending on context [8].
- Artistic integration: Hieroglyphs were often incorporated into Maya art, blending text and image in complex ways [9].
- Calligraphic variation: Scribes had considerable freedom in how they rendered individual signs, leading to regional and temporal variations in style [10].
- Phonetic complementation: Logograms were often accompanied by phonetic signs to clarify pronunciation or grammatical information [11].

One of the most intriguing aspects of Maya writing is its use of conflation and infixation, where multiple signs could be combined into a single glyph block, creating visually complex but linguistically efficient constructions [12].

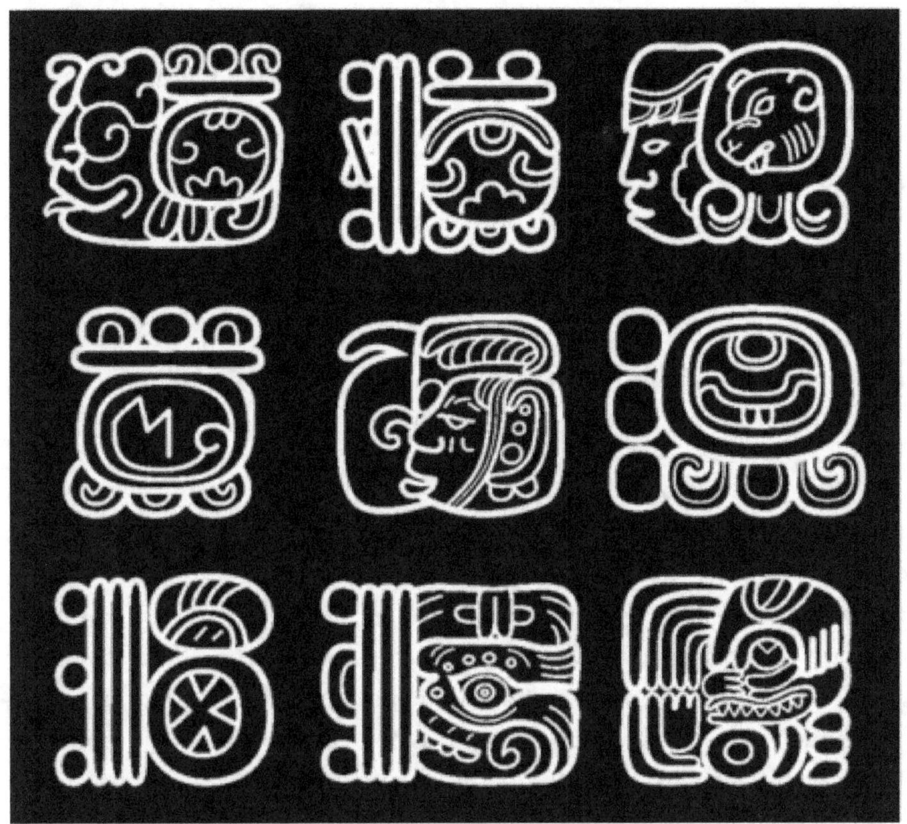

Maya hieroglyphic writing

The Maya hieroglyphic corpus

The corpus of Maya hieroglyphic texts is extensive and diverse, although much has been lost due to the tropical climate and historical events. The surviving corpus includes:

- Monumental inscriptions on stone stelae, altars, and building facades
- Painted texts on ceramics and murals
- Inscriptions on portable objects like jade ornaments and bones
- Four surviving pre-Columbian codices (folding books)
- Colonial-era documents that preserve hieroglyphic traditions [13].

The total number of known hieroglyphic texts is difficult to quantify precisely, but it is estimated to be in the tens of thousands. However, many of these are fragmentary or consist of only a few glyphs [14].

These texts are scattered across museums, archaeological sites, and private collections worldwide. Major collections can be found in:

- The National Museum of Anthropology in Mexico City
- The Museo Popol Vuh in Guatemala City
- The Peabody Museum at Harvard University
- The British Museum in London [15].

The *Dresden Codex* is one of the few surviving pre-Columbian Maya books, dating back to the 11th or 12th century CE. Originally created in Yucatán, Mexico, it was later taken to Europe and is now preserved in Dresden, Germany, hence its name. The *Codex* consists of 39 double-sided sheets made from amate paper, featuring hieroglyphic text and colorful illustrations. Its contents primarily focus on astronomical calculations, calendrical information, and religious rituals, including instructions for ceremonies and prophecies. The *Dresden Codex* is particularly notable for its detailed Venus tables, which track the planet's movements with remarkable accuracy. This manuscript is of immense importance to scholars, as it provides invaluable insights into Maya mathematics, astronomy, religion, and daily life, serving as a crucial source for understanding this ancient Mesoamerican civilization [16].

Preservation and conservation

The preservation of Maya hieroglyphic texts presents significant challenges. Stone monuments have often suffered from weathering, vandalism, or looting. Painted texts on ceramics and plaster are particularly vulnerable to degradation. The humid tropical environment of much of the Maya area has not been conducive to the preservation of organic materials, which is why so few codices have survived [17].

Modern conservation efforts employ a range of techniques to preserve and study Maya inscriptions, including:

- 3D scanning and photogrammetry of monuments
- Multispectral imaging to reveal faded paint on ceramics and codices
- Laser cleaning of stone monuments
- Climate-controlled storage for fragile artifacts [18].

Digital preservation has become increasingly important, with projects like the Maya Hieroglyphic Database working to create comprehensive digital corpora of Maya texts [19].

Societal use of Maya hieroglyphs

Maya hieroglyphs played a crucial role in Maya society, serving multiple functions:

- <u>Historical records</u>: Many monumental inscriptions record dynastic histories, wars, alliances, and other significant events [20].
- <u>Calendrical and astronomical texts</u>: The Maya were skilled astronomers, and many texts deal with calendrical calculations and astronomical observations [21].
- <u>Religious and ritual texts</u>: Hieroglyphs were used to record religious beliefs, mythological narratives, and ritual practices [22].
- <u>Elite communication</u>: The ability to read and write hieroglyphs was largely restricted to the elite class, including rulers, priests, and scribes [23].
- <u>Economic records</u>: Some texts, particularly on ceramics, record economic transactions or denote ownership [24].
- <u>Personal names and titles</u>: Many inscriptions simply record the names and titles of individuals, often in connection with specific events or objects [25].

The use of hieroglyphs was closely tied to Maya concepts of time and cyclical history. Many texts begin with elaborate calendar notations, situating events within multiple cycles of time [26].

Decipherment and translation challenges

The decipherment of Maya hieroglyphs is one of the great intellectual achievements of the 20th century. Unlike Egyptian hieroglyphs or cuneiform, Maya writing had no clear descendants at the time of European contact, making its decipherment particularly challenging [27].

Key breakthroughs in decipherment include:

- Yuri Knorozov's phonetic approach in the 1950s
- Tatiana Proskouriakoff's identification of historical content in the 1960s
- The Palenque Round Table meetings beginning in 1973, which brought together scholars to share findings [28].

Despite these advances, challenges in translation persist:

- <u>Linguistic diversity</u>: The Maya area encompassed multiple languages, and texts from different regions or time periods may reflect different linguistic features [29].
- <u>Metaphorical language</u>: Many Maya texts use highly metaphorical language that can be difficult to interpret without a deep understanding of Maya culture [30].
- <u>Damaged or eroded texts</u>: Many inscriptions are partially destroyed or weathered, making complete readings impossible [31].
- <u>Limited corpus for certain periods</u>: Some time periods or regions are underrepresented in the surviving corpus, creating gaps in our understanding [32].

While the majority of Maya texts can now be read phonetically, debate continues over the interpretation of certain passages, particularly those dealing with religious or metaphysical concepts [33].

Application of AI to Maya hieroglyphic studies

In recent years, artificial intelligence (AI) and machine learning techniques have begun to be applied to the study of Maya hieroglyphs. While these applications are still in their early stages, several promising projects have emerged:

- <u>Automated glyph recognition</u>: Researchers at the University of Stuttgart have developed machine learning algorithms to automatically identify Maya glyphs from photographs of inscriptions [34].
- <u>Pattern analysis</u>: AI is being used to analyze patterns in glyph usage across different sites and time periods, potentially revealing new insights into scribal practices and regional variations [35].
- <u>Damaged text reconstruction</u>: Machine learning models are being developed to assist in reconstructing partially damaged texts based on context and known patterns [36].
- <u>Digital paleography</u>: AI techniques are being applied to the study of scribal hands and stylistic variations in Maya writing [37].

Potential for further AI applications

The potential for further use of AI in Maya hieroglyphic studies is significant. Some promising areas for future research include:

- <u>Corpus expansion</u>: As new Maya texts are discovered or made accessible, AI could assist in quickly identifying, transcribing, and categorizing them, expanding the corpus available for study [38].
- <u>Contextual analysis</u>: Advanced natural language processing techniques could be used to analyze the context and content of Maya inscriptions, potentially revealing new patterns or associations in the texts [39].
- <u>Cross-disciplinary integration</u>: AI could help integrate data from epigraphy, archaeology, and other fields to provide a more holistic understanding of Maya texts in their cultural context [40].
- <u>Translation assistance</u>: While fully automated translation of Maya texts is not currently feasible, AI could potentially assist human translators by suggesting possible readings for unclear or damaged sections of text [41].

- <u>Comparative studies</u>: AI could facilitate large-scale comparisons between Maya writing and other Mesoamerican scripts, potentially shedding light on cultural interactions and influences [42].
- <u>Predictive modeling</u>: Machine learning models could be used to predict likely content of damaged or missing portions of texts based on known patterns and contextual information [43].

Challenges and ethical considerations

While the application of AI to Maya hieroglyphic studies offers exciting possibilities, it also presents challenges and ethical considerations:

- <u>Data quality</u>: The effectiveness of AI analysis depends on the quality and comprehensiveness of the input data. Ensuring accurate digitization and transcription of Maya texts is crucial [44].
- <u>Interpretative bias</u>: AI systems may inadvertently incorporate or amplify existing biases in how researchers interpret Maya texts. Careful design and critical evaluation of AI models is essential [45].
- <u>Cultural sensitivity</u>: The study of Maya writing involves engaging with the cultural heritage of living Maya communities. It's important that AI applications in this field respect and involve these communities [46].
- <u>Access and ownership</u>: As digital corpora and AI models are developed, questions arise about who owns this data and how it should be shared among researchers, Maya communities, and the public [47].
- <u>Ethical AI development</u>: Ensuring that AI development in this field adheres to ethical guidelines, including transparency and replicability of results, is crucial for maintaining scientific integrity [48].

Conclusion

The study of Maya hieroglyphs continues to yield fascinating insights into one of the most sophisticated civilizations of the ancient Americas. From monumental inscriptions that have stood for millennia to the fragile pages of the surviving codices, these texts offer a window into a rich and complex culture that flourished for over a thousand years.

As we move forward, the integration of traditional scholarly methods with advanced AI technologies offers new hope for deepening our understanding of Maya writing and the civilization that produced it. However, it's crucial that this technological progress is balanced with a deep respect for the cultural significance of these ancient texts and a commitment to ethical and inclusive research practices.

The decipherment of Maya hieroglyphs in the 20th century revolutionized our understanding of ancient American history. Perhaps the application of AI in the 21st century will lead to equally transformative discoveries, unlocking new secrets about Maya language, culture, and history. As we continue to explore these ancient writings, we not only learn about the Maya past but also gain insights into the enduring legacy of this remarkable civilization.

<u>References</u>

[1] Coe, M. D. (2012). *Breaking the Maya Code*. Thames and Hudson, p. 9.

[2] Sharer, R. J., & Traxler, L. P. (2006). *The Ancient Maya* (6th ed.). Stanford University Press. Available on the Internet Archive.

[3] Houston, S. D. (Ed.). (2004). *The First Writing: Script Invention as History and Process*. Cambridge University Press.

[4] Justeson, J. S., & Kaufman, T. (1993). A Decipherment of Epi-Olmec Hieroglyphic Writing. *Science*, 259(5102), 1703-1711.

[5] Martin, S., & Grube, N. (2008). *Chronicle of the Maya Kings and Queens: Deciphering the Dynasties of the Ancient Maya* (2nd ed.). Thames & Hudson.

[6] Law, D. (2014). *Language Contact, Inherited Similarity and Social Difference: The Story of Linguistic Interaction in the Maya Lowlands*. John Benjamins Publishing Company.

[7] Kettunen, H., & Helmke, C. (2020). *Introduction to Maya Hieroglyphs* (19th ed.). Wayeb.

[8] Houston, S. D., Robertson, J., & Stuart, D. (2000). The Language of Classic Maya Inscriptions. *Current Anthropology*, 41(3), 321-356.

[9] Stone, A., & Zender, M. (2011). *Reading Maya Art: A Hieroglyphic Guide to Ancient Maya Painting and Sculpture*. Thames & Hudson.

[10] Stuart, D. (2011). *The Order of Days: The Maya World and the Truth About 2012*. Doubleday Religion.

[11] Stuart, D. (1987). *Ten Phonetic Syllables. Research Reports on Ancient Maya Writing No.14*. Center for Maya Research, Washington DC.

[12] Macri, M. J., & Looper, M. G. (2003). *The New Catalog of Maya Hieroglyphs, Volume 1: The Classic Period Inscriptions*. University of Oklahoma Press.

[13] Houston, S. D. & Inomata, T. (2009). *The Classic Maya*. Cambridge University Press.

[14] Graham, I. (1975). *Corpus of Maya Hieroglyphic Inscriptions, Volume 1: Introduction to the Corpus*. Peabody Museum of Archaeology and Ethnology, Harvard University Press.

[15] Schele, L., & Miller, M. E. (1986). *The Blood of Kings: Dynasty and Ritual in Maya Art*. Kimbell Art Museum. George Braziller.

[16] Vail, G., & Aveni, A. (Eds.). (2006). The Madrid Codex: New Approaches to Understanding an Ancient Maya Manuscript. *Journal of Latin American Anthropology*, 11(1), 222-224.

[17] Houston, S. D., Chinchilla Mazariegos, O., & Stuart, D. (Eds.). (2001). *The Decipherment of Ancient Maya Writing*. University of Oklahoma Press.

[18] Tokovinine, A., & Fash, B. (2014). Scanning History: The Corpus of Maya Hieroglyphic Inscriptions Tests a 3-D Scanner in the Field. *Symbols*, Spring (2008), 17-20.

[19] Vail, G., & Macri, M. J. (2012). *The New Catalog of Maya Hieroglyphs, Volume Two: Codical Texts* (Vol. 264). University of Oklahoma Press.

[20] Martin, S., & Grube, N. (2008). *Chronicle of the Maya Kings and Queens: Deciphering the Dynasties of the Ancient Maya*. Thames & Hudson.

[21] Rice, P. M. (2007). *Maya Calendar Origins: Monuments, Mythistory, and the Materialization of Time*. University of Texas Press.

[22] Coe, M. D., & Van Stone, M. (2005). *Reading the Maya Glyphs* (2nd ed.). Thames & Hudson.

[23] Houston, S. D., & Stuart, D. (1996). Of Gods, Glyphs and Kings: Divinity and Rulership among the Classic Maya. *Antiquity*, 70(268), 289-312.

[24] Reents-Budet, D. (1994). *Painting the Maya Universe: Royal Ceramics of the Classic Period*. Duke University Press.

[25] Stuart, D. (2005). *The Inscriptions from Temple XIX at Palenque: A Commentary*. Pre-Columbian Art Research Institute.

[26] Aveni, A. F. (2001). *Skywatchers: A Revised and Updated Version of Skywatchers of Ancient Mexico*. University of Texas Press.

[27] Coe, M. D. (1992). *Breaking the Maya Code*. Thames and Hudson.

[28] Houston, S. D., Chinchilla Mazariegos, O., & Stuart, D. (Eds.). (2001). *The Decipherment of Ancient Maya Writing*. University of Oklahoma Press.

[29] Law, D. (2014). *Language Contact, Inherited Similarity and Social Difference: The Story of Linguistic Interaction in the Maya Lowlands*. John Benjamins Publishing Company.

[30] Hull, K. M. (2003). *Verbal Art and Performance in Ch'orti' and Maya Hieroglyphic Writing*. University of Texas at Austin.

[31] Stuart, D. (1996). Kings of Stone: A Consideration of Stelae in Ancient Maya Ritual and Representation. *RES: Anthropology and Aesthetics*, 29(1), 148-171.

[32] Grube, N. K., Eggebrecht, E., & Seidel, M. (2007). *Maya: Divine kings of the rain forest*. Könemann.

[33] Houston, S. D., Robertson, J., & Stuart, D. (2000). The Language of Classic Maya Inscriptions. *Current Anthropology*, 41(3), 321-356.

[34] Maaten, L. V. D., Buti, L., Díaz-Herrera, J., Ghezzi, I., & Mara, H. (2017). Computer Vision and Machine Learning for Archaeology. *Journal on Computing and Cultural Heritage*, 10(1), 1-5.

[35] Zimmermann, G., Schön, S., & Mara, H. (2018). Automatic Analysis of Maya Hieroglyphs using CNN and LSTM Networks. In *2018 IEEE International Conference on Artificial Intelligence and Virtual Reality (AIVR)* (pp. 193-196). IEEE.

[36] Russakovsky, O., Deng, J., Su, H., Krause, J., Satheesh, S., Ma, S., ... & Fei-Fei, L. (2015). ImageNet Large Scale Visual Recognition Challenge. *International Journal of Computer Vision*, 115(3), 211-252.

[37] Oonk, S., & Spijker, J. (2015). A Supervised Machine-Learning Approach Towards Geochemical Predictive Modeling in Archaeology. *Journal of Archaeological Science*, 59, 80-88.

[38] Kampel, M. & Sablatnig, R. (2005). Robust 3D Reconstruction of Archaeological Pottery based on Concentric Circular Rills. In *Proceedings of the 6th International Workshop on Image Analysis for Multimedia Interactive Services (WIAMIS'05)* (pp. 14-20).

[39] Manning, C. D., & Schütze, H. (1999). *Foundations of Statistical Natural Language Processing*. MIT Press.

[40] Bevan, A., & Lake, M. (Eds.). (2016). *Computational Approaches to Archaeological Spaces*. Routledge.

[41] Shaus, A., Turkel, E., & Piasetzky, E. (2017). Binarization of First Temple Period Inscriptions: Performance of Existing Algorithms and a New Registration Based Scheme. In *2017 14th IAPR International Conference on Document Analysis and Recognition (ICDAR)* (Vol. 1, pp. 21-26). IEEE.

[42] Bevan, A. (2015). The Data Deluge. *Antiquity*, 89(348), 1473-1484.

[43] Graham, S., Weingart, S., & Milligan, I. (2012). Getting Started with Topic Modeling and MALLET. *Programming Historian.* https://doi.org/10.46430/phen0017

[44] Terras, M. M. (2006). *Image to Interpretation: An Intelligent System to Aid Historians in Reading the Vindolanda Texts.* Oxford University Press.

[45] Caliskan, A., Bryson, J. J., & Narayanan, A. (2017). Semantics Derived Automatically from Language Corpora Contain Human-like Biases. *Science*, 356(6334), 183-186.

[46] Jackson, J. E. (2005). *The Story of Writing: Alphabets, Hieroglyphs & Pictograms.* Thames & Hudson.

[47] Cuno, J., & Weiss, L. (Eds.). (2020). Cultural Heritage Under Siege. *J Paul Getty Trust Occasional Papers In Cultural Heritage Policy. No.4.*

[48] Jobin, A., Ienca, M., & Vayena, E. (2019). The Global Landscape of AI Ethics Guidelines. *Nature Machine Intelligence*, 1(9), 389-399.

[49] Crist, W., Shaus, A., Sober, B., Turkel, E., & Piasetzky, E. (2019). Integrating Artificial Intelligence into Archaeological Research: A Case Study from Tel Megiddo. *Journal of Archaeological Science: Reports*, 27, 101971.

[50] Terras, M. (2016). Crowdsourcing in the Digital Humanities. In S. Schreibman, R. Siemens, & J. Unsworth (Eds.), *A New Companion to Digital Humanities* (pp. 420-439). Wiley-Blackwell.

[51] Faigenbaum-Golovin, S., Shaus, A., Sober, B., Turkel, E., Piasetzky, E., & Finkelstein, I. (2020). Potential for Machine Learning in Digital Epigraphy: ML-Assisted Reconstruction of Biblical Hebrew Inscriptions. *Digital Scholarship in the Humanities*, 35(2), 361-375.

[52] Hsiang, J., & Mendoza, R. G. (2016). Paleoclimate Reconstruction and Pollen-Climate Response Surfaces for Mexico and Guatemala. *Journal of Archaeological Science: Reports*, 7, 130-139.

[53] Bonacchi, C., Bevan, A., Pett, D., Keinan-Schoonbaert, A., Sparks, R., Wexler, J., & Wilkin, N. (2014). Crowd-sourced Archaeological Research: The MicroPasts Project. *Archaeology International*, 17, 61-68. https://doi.org/10.5334/ai.1705

CHAPTER TWELVE

The enduring significance of ancient languages and scripts

Language is the archives of history, Ralph Waldo Emerson, 'The Collected Works'.
[1]

The study of ancient languages and scripts is not merely an academic pursuit — it is a key to understanding the very foundations of human civilization. Throughout history, written language has been a means for societies to record their achievements, beliefs, and identities. From the earliest cuneiform tablets of the Sumerians to the enigmatic glyphs of the Maya, the development of script has allowed us to bridge the gap between the ancient past and the present. Yet, despite the significant advancements in deciphering many ancient scripts, several remain mysteries, and with them, untold stories of human ingenuity and history remain locked away.

Language as a cornerstone of civilization

The development of written language marked a turning point in human history. The ability to encode complex ideas, laws, religious texts, and economic transactions allowed early civilizations to build complex societies that could sustain themselves over centuries. In places like Mesopotamia, Egypt, and the Indus Valley, the written word became a medium for transmitting culture, governing expansive empires, and documenting the relationships between humans and their gods. Language became the vessel for preserving knowledge, whether that was scientific, religious, or philosophical, and it remains the most important tool we have to understand what ancient peoples knew and valued.

Deciphered scripts such as Akkadian, Sumerian, and Egyptian hieroglyphs have revealed remarkable insights into the lives and thoughts of ancient civilizations. Sumerian texts on astronomy, for instance, have shown us that their knowledge of the heavens was advanced beyond what we had previously imagined, influencing later civilizations like the Babylonians and even the

Greeks [2]. Egyptian hieroglyphs have provided us with a window into the intricate and deeply spiritual world of the Pharaohs, offering a glimpse into their sophisticated belief systems, governance, and relationships with the natural world [3].

But for all that we have uncovered, the work remains incomplete. The undeciphered scripts—such as the Indus Valley script, Linear A, and the enigmatic language of the Etruscans—are tantalizing reminders of the knowledge that still eludes us. Each undeciphered text represents a missing piece of the puzzle, a barrier to fully understanding the achievements, innovations, and wisdom of the societies that wrote them. It is as if we are only hearing fragments of a much larger conversation, and without unlocking these remaining scripts, much of what the ancients knew remains lost to history.

The implications of undeciphered languages

The significance of the undeciphered languages cannot be overstated. For example, the people of the Indus Valley were contemporaries of the Egyptians and Mesopotamians, yet their culture and accomplishments remain largely obscure due to our inability to read their writing. Scholars have uncovered extensive urban planning, evidence of trade, and intricate craftsmanship, but without the key to their written language, much of the socio-political, religious, and scientific aspects of their society remain hidden [4]. What does their writing tell us about their worldview, their technological advancements, or their relationships with neighboring civilizations? These questions continue to drive researchers to unlock the secrets of the Indus Valley script.

Similarly, the language of Linear A, used by the Minoans on Crete, presents another challenge. Though Linear B, a script used by Mycenaean Greeks, has been deciphered and revealed much about their bureaucratic systems and economy, Linear A has so far defied decipherment. This means that the earlier Minoan civilization, one of Europe's oldest, remains obscured from our understanding. What insights about their religion, governance, and culture lie in the undeciphered texts of Linear A? If we could read these writings, they would likely shed light on one of the formative cultures of the ancient Mediterranean and its influence on later Greek civilization [5].

The loss of knowledge due to undeciphered scripts affects not only our understanding of individual civilizations but also the broader picture of human development. Many of these ancient cultures were interconnected through trade, diplomacy, and conflict. Phoenician, for example, was an important bridge language in the ancient world, facilitating trade across the Mediterranean and influencing the development of the Greek alphabet, which in turn shaped Latin and the scripts we use today [6]. Without full comprehension of the lesser-understood scripts, we are missing essential details about these early global networks, which were instrumental in the spread of technology, ideas, and cultures.

The role of script development in modern society

The development of ancient scripts has a profound impact on modern society, as it is through these early languages that the structure of modern communication was born. The process of transforming spoken language into a visual, written form allowed ideas to be recorded and preserved across generations, giving birth to the concept of history itself. This lineage can be seen clearly in the Phoenician alphabet, which gave rise to the Greek and Latin scripts that are the direct ancestors of many modern writing systems. Every time we write in a Latin-based script, we are partaking in a tradition that stretches back millennia to the ancient scribes of the Near East and Mediterranean [7].

Moreover, the study of ancient languages has revealed the surprising complexity of early societies. The scripts that have been deciphered and translated tell us that these ancient people were not simply primitive precursors to modernity, but sophisticated, technologically advanced cultures in their own right. Their achievements in mathematics, astronomy, architecture, and law have had a lasting influence on subsequent civilizations, including our own. The Maya, for instance, developed a calendar system that was incredibly accurate and continues to fascinate scholars for its precision and complexity [8].

Beyond the purely academic pursuit, deciphering ancient scripts allows us to reclaim lost knowledge, which can have practical applications today. For example, ancient medical texts from Egypt and Mesopotamia have informed modern understanding of herbal medicine and surgical practices [9].

Understanding how ancient cultures approached problems such as urban planning, agriculture, and governance can also provide fresh perspectives on modern challenges.

Why deciphering ancient languages matters

The field of deciphering ancient languages and scripts holds immense potential for uncovering not only the histories of specific civilizations but also the shared history of humanity. Each breakthrough in deciphering brings us closer to understanding the intricacies of how early societies developed, how they interacted with one another, and how their ideas evolved over time. It is through these ancient languages that we learn not only about past societies but also about the fundamental aspects of human culture and cognition.

At the heart of this endeavor lies a profound philosophical question: What have we lost as a result of our inability to read certain ancient texts? What knowledge, wisdom, or philosophical insights have vanished into the annals of time because we cannot yet unlock the written words of the Indus Valley, Linear A, or the Etruscans? The quest to decipher these languages is not merely about solving puzzles; it is about reclaiming the intellectual and cultural heritage of humanity as a whole.

Conclusion

In sum, the development of ancient languages and scripts represents one of the most critical junctures in the history of human civilization. From the early cuneiform of Sumer to the mysterious glyphs of the Maya, written language has shaped the course of history by enabling the preservation and transmission of ideas across generations. Deciphering these ancient scripts provides us with valuable insights into the cultures, beliefs, and achievements of past civilizations, and those that remain undeciphered represent tantalizing mysteries that continue to motivate scholars around the world.

The study of these languages is not only an academic pursuit but also a search for the collective memory of humanity. Each discovery brings us closer to understanding the roots of our own civilization, the interconnectedness of ancient peoples, and the shared heritage that underpins the modern world.

The importance of this branch of archaeology cannot be overstated—our understanding of the past is continually deepened and enriched through the painstaking work of deciphering and translating these ancient languages.

<u>References</u>

[1] Emerson, R. W. (1883). *The Collected Works of Ralph Waldo Emerson.* Houghton Mifflin, p. 214.

[2] Steele, J. M. (2012). *Ancient Mesopotamian Astronomy and Its Impact on Later Civilizations.* Oxford University Press, p. 120.

[3] Wilkinson, R. H. (2016). *The Complete Gods and Goddesses of Ancient Egypt.* Thames & Hudson, p. 85.

[4] Kenoyer, J. M. (2005). *The Indus Valley Civilization: A Contemporary Perspective.* University of Pennsylvania Press, p. 72.

[5] Chadwick, J. (1990). *The Decipherment of Linear B.* Cambridge University Press, p. 45.

[6] Baurain, C. (2014). Phoenician Influence on Mediterranean Writing Systems. *Journal of Near Eastern Studies*, Vol. 73, pp. 29-56.

[7] Daniels, P. T. (1996). *The World's Writing Systems.* Oxford University Press, p. 139.

[8] Tedlock, D. (1992). *Time and the Highland Maya.* University of New Mexico Press, p. 23.

[9] Nunn, J. F. (2002). *Ancient Egyptian Medicine.* University of Oklahoma Press, p. 59.

◉

AUTHOR

John Gillam

Independent Writer On Antiquity

John brings a fresh and enlightening perspective to the topic of ancient civilizations. With a career as a librarian at the prestigious National Library of Australia and extensive experience in the Public Service, he combines meticulous research skills with a deep understanding of human nature and societal structures.

His series of books on *Decoding Antiquity* goes beyond mere historical recounting, instead providing profound insights into what we can learn from our ancient ancestors and the events that shaped their lives.

In this book, *Translating Ancient Texts*, John tracks the ingenious development of ancient alphabets and writings, and explores the enormous amount of work

TRANSLATING ANCIENT TEXTS

that has gone into deciphering and translating ancient texts. However, many of these texts still lie in museums and archives, undeciphered and untranslated. What information lies waiting to be revealed? What knowledge did the ancients possess that we have forgotten or never contemplated? Could artificial intelligence help to speed the deciphering and translation process?

Translating Ancient Texts offers readers a captivating journey through time, language, and human ingenuity, revealing the ongoing quest to understand our past and how it shapes our present and future.

Contact: John-Gillam@bigpond.com

www.decodingantiquity.weebly.com